CHALLENGED
BY
The New Testament

E. KEITH HOWICK

Other Books by E. Keith Howick

The *Challenged by the Bible* Series

CHALLENGED BY The New Testament

E. KEITH HOWICK

WindRiver Publishing
St. George, Utah

Queries, comments or correspondence concerning this work should be directed to the author and submitted to WindRiver Publishing at:

authors@windriverpublishing.com

Information regarding this work or other works published by WindRiver Publishing, Inc., and instructions for submitting manuscripts for review for publication, can be found at:

www.windriverpublishing.com

Challenged by the New Testament

Library of Congress Control Number: 2004094219
ISBN 1-886249-23-7

First Printing 2004

Printed in the U.S.A. by Malloy, Inc., on acid-free paper

Table of Contents

List of Abbreviations

Matt.	The Gospel According to St. Matthew
Mark	The Gospel According to St. Mark
Luke	The Gospel According to St. Luke
John	The Gospel According to St. John
Acts	The Acts of the Apostles
Rom.	The Epistle of Paul the Apostle to the Romans
1 Cor.	The First Epistle of Paul the Apostle to the Corinthians
2 Cor.	The Second Epistle of Paul the Apostle to the Corinthians
Gal.	The Epistle of Paul the Apostle to the Galatians
Eph.	The Epistle of Paul the Apostle to the Ephesians
Philip.	The Epistle of Paul the Apostle to the Philippians
Col.	The Epistle of Paul the Apostle to The Colossians
1 Thes.	The First Epistle of Paul the Apostle to the Thessalonians
2 Thes.	The Second Epistle of Paul the Apostle to the Thessalonians
1 Tim.	The First Epistle of Paul the Apostle to Timothy
2 Tim.	The Second Epistle of Paul the Apostle to Timothy
Titus	The Epistle of Paul to Titus
Philem.	The Epistle of Paul to Philemon
Heb.	The Epistle of Paul the Apostle to the Hebrews
James	The General Epistle of James
1 Pet.	The First Epistle General of Peter
2 Pet.	The Second Epistle General of Peter
1 John	The First Epistle General of John
2 John	The Second Epistle of John
3 John	The Third Epistle of John
Jude	The General Epistle of Jude
Rev.	The Revelation of St. John the Divine

List of Puzzles and Games

Match Games

Miscellaneous Games

The New Testament is a unique book of scripture. While it is a unit unto itself, it is also a compilation of individual books: Gospels, Acts (a historical continuation of the Gospel of Luke), multiple Epistles, and the book of Revelation. Some of the writers were eye witnesses to the Lord's work and some were gatherers of information or missionaries of the new gospel, but all were determined to witness and testify that the Savior of the world had come. The New Testament is a well of living water that provides the serious student with enormous quantities of material to aid in his or her quest for eternal life in the kingdom of God. It is a powerful witness of the divinity of Jesus Christ, but it also contains advice, doctrine, and instruction pertaining to the path of Salvation. However, even though all the material contained in the scriptural record is serious and important, you can have fun while you learn the information contained between its covers.

Challenged by the New Testament uses the King James Version of the Bible as the source of its material, not because it is better than any other translation, but because it is the first widely distributed English translation. Various Christian groups or individuals may prefer another translation of the Bible, but since the King James version is commonly known and readily available, it was my text of choice for this educational activity book.

There are more than twenty-four hundred questions contained in this book. Each question comes from the pages of the New Testament, or in a few instances, from general knowledge about the traditions concerning it. The reader will find several particularly interesting questions on the "Start" and "Finale" pages and in the "Conclusion" of the book, but regardless of where they're located, every question has an answer provided and a scriptural reference to verify the answer. The reference will generally come after the question to allow the reader to find the answer by looking up the scripture—before peeking at the answer (although in some instances the reference will be in the answer rather than after the question). Nonetheless, all answers—both for the games and the questions—can be found in the "Answers" section at the end of the book.

This book is divided into ten Sections. Each Section contains topical headings and multiple games (a list of the games is provided in the Table of Contents). The sections, headings, categories, arrangement, and placement of the questions are my own. They are meant to help parents, students, teachers, and ecclesiastical leaders increase their personal enjoyment, as well as to supplement their lessons and other activities. This book has a simple goal—to teach the New Testament in an interesting way.

So have fun. Take the quiz of a lifetime from the New Testament. Enjoy discovering new things from this unique and marvelous work. And if you find that you can answer all of these questions without peeking, you are more than just a scholar, you're a genius!

Happy Quizzing!

As you begin your trek into the New Testament, you will discover multiple occasions that identify Jesus as the Son of God. Six of these are very unique.

Question: On three specific occasions Jesus testified to the people, or to the Jewish leadership, that He was the anticipated Messiah. The results were the same—they tried to kill Him. Can you name these occasions?

Answer: These three testimonies came:

a. in a synagogue in Nazareth when He read from Isaiah 61:1–2 (a recognized Messianic prophecy), and said: "This day is this scripture fulfilled in your ears;" (Luke 4:16–30)

b. in the "Light of the World" discourse and the discussion with the Jewish leadership that followed; (John 8; particularly 8:58–59)

c. in the "Good Shepherd" discourse and the discussion that followed. (John 10:24, 30–39)

The other three occasions that identify Christ as the Son of God are incorporated into your first official question—and it's a hard one.

1. Three times the Father spoke from the heavens testifying of, or responding to his Son. Name the occasions. (Matt. 3:17; Matt. 17:5; John 12:28–29)

Now we can begin in earnest.

And The Word Was Made Flesh

2. In John, Jesus declared God to be a what? (John 4:24)

3. To know the only true God, and Jesus Christ whom He sent is to have what? (John 17:3)

4. What must the Father do for men to come unto Jesus? (John 6:44)

5. The Father gave Jesus power to have life in whom? (John 5:26)

6. According to Paul, God is not the author of what? (1 Cor. 14:33)

7. What does Paul say all men have done that causes them to come short of the glory of God? (Rom. 3:23)

8. The Father has life in what person? (John 5:26)

9. James declares that you are an enemy of God if you are a friend to what? (James 4:4)

10. Who did Jesus say has seen the Father? (John 6:46)

11. Paul taught that without what, it is impossible to please God? (Heb. 11:6)

12. What was the inscription on the altar Paul used to teach the Athenians? (Acts 17:23)

13. No man knoweth the things of God, but by the what? (1 Cor. 2:11)

14. For God so loved the world that He gave His what? (John 3:16)

15. Paul stated there was one God and one what, between God and man? (1 Tim. 2:5)

16. Jesus declared that God is not the God of the dead, but of the what? (Matt. 22:32)

17. In the first verse of John's Gospel he defines God as the what? (John 1:1)

18. Paul declared to the Ephesians that God had chosen "us" before the foundation of the what? (Eph. 1:4)

19. In Hebrews, Paul declared that God, through His Son made what orbs? (Heb. 1:2)

20. Paul said that what God has promised, He is able to what? (Rom. 4:21)

Trick Question

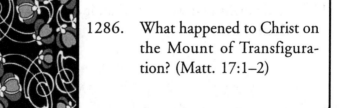

1286. What happened to Christ on the Mount of Transfiguration? (Matt. 17:1–2)

46. Jesus taught that when the Comforter comes, he will "reprove" the world of righteousness, of judgment, and of what? (John 16:8)

47. What did Jesus designate as another name for the Holy Ghost? (John 14:26)

48. The Holy Ghost was first manifest to the Apostles (after the resurrection of Jesus) on what day? (Acts 2:1–4)

49. Who offered the Apostles money for the power to confer the Holy Ghost? (Acts 8:9, 18)

50. What was the result of Sapphira tempting the Holy Ghost when she lied to Peter? (Acts 5:9–10)

51. The Holy Ghost was one, but Jesus promised the Apostles that He would pray to the Father to send another what? (John 14:16)

52. How did the Apostles give the Holy Ghost to new converts? (Acts 8:17)

53. The Spirit directed Philip to teach what man as the man rode in his coach? (Acts 8:27)

THE GODHEAD
And The Word Was Made Flesh

Solution on page 281

Across

1 The wise men came from this direction to see the baby Jesus. (Matt. 2:1)

3 Because Jesus came eating and drinking, they called Him gluttonous and a what? (Matt. 11:19)

5 Paul said that if Christ be not raised, thls synonym for belief is in vain. (1 Cor 15:17)

6 After His birth, the baby Jesus was laid in this. (Luke 2:12)

8 Paul taught that the Son was made of this human "under the law." (Gal. 4:4)

10 As a result of Ananias lying to the Holy Ghost, he "gave up the ghost," which means he _____. (Acts 5:5)

14 Paul taught that we can become reconciled with God if we slay this form of hatred. (Eph. 2:16)

15 The Father is the husbandman, and Jesus is the true what? (John 15:1)

16 Paul declares that God is not (or will not be) this. (Gal. 6:7)

17 Paul taught that if we live in the Spirit, we should also do this in the Spirit. (Gal. 5:25)

19 Paul said that the foolishness of God is wiser than the wisdom of these (His creations). (1 Cor. 1:25)

20 Simon the sorcerer offered the Apostles this, if they would give him the

power to confer the Holy Ghost. (Acts 8:18)

21 Paul taught that Christ, risen from the dead of all who slept, became like these first picked from the tree. (1 Cor. 15:20)

22 John states that whosoever is born of God does not commit this breaking of the law. (1 John 3:9)

25 Matthew records that by the time the wise men came to see Jesus, He was living in this type of an abode. (Matt. 2:11)

27 Paul states that Christ is preached whether in truth or this simile for deception. (Philip. 1:18)

29 Paul taught in Hebrews that Jesus is in the brightness and image of this Supreme Being. (Heb. 1:1–3)

31 The Son of God was manifested to destroy the works of this evil opposite. (1 John 3:8)

32 Jesus said that if you do the Father's will, you will know of this type of teaching. (John 7:17)

33 John used this name for Jesus when he said Jesus had made all things. (John 1:1–3)

35 This is the name of the person who is in the image of the invisible God. (Col. 1:15 (13–18))

36 This is the town where Jesus was born. (Matt. 2:1)

Down

2 Paul taught that though a Son, yet Jesus learned obedience by the things which He what? (Heb. 5:8)

3 Paul said that he planted, Apollos performed this nourishing act, and God gave the increase. (1 Cor. 3:6)

4 Jesus used this title/name with the Jews. It indicated that He was before Abraham. (John 8:58)

7 John declares in his general Epistle that God is this emotion. (1 John 4:8)

9 The Holy Ghost forbade Paul to preach the word in this general area. (Acts 16:6)

11 God chooses the foolish things to confound things that men think are this. (1 Cor. 1:27)

12 Mark declares that because of this state of mind of his countrymen, Jesus could do no mighty works in his own country. (Mark 6:5–6)

13 Paul said because the Greeks loved logic, Christ seemed like this (opposite of logic) to them. (1 Cor. 1:23)

18 Jesus declared that He was the way, the truth, and the what? (John 14:6)

22 When Jesus walked on the water, He was thought to be this apparition. (Matt. 14:26)

23 Paul said we should not do this to the Spirit of God. (Eph. 4:30)

24 If you labor and are heavy laden, Jesus will give you this peaceful state. (Matt. 11:28)

26 Paul taught that through faith, these orbs were framed by God. (Heb. 11:3)

28 According to Jesus, who is our Master? (Matt. 23:10)

30 The Spirit of God descended upon Jesus like this bird. (Matt. 3:16)

34 Jesus said that He and his Father were represented by this single unit. (John 10:30)

21. What major entrance, is described in John 12?

22. If we have seen Jesus, we have seen what person? (John 14:9)

23. What was the Pharisee's answer to the questions: "What think ye of Christ? Whose son is he?" (Matt. 22:42)

24. In John, Chapter 1, John calls Jesus the what? (John 1:1)

25. What is the book, chapter, and verse telling of Jesus' growth and status among men from birth to age twelve?

26. What was the reaction of the people at Nazareth when Jesus declared his divinity to them? (Luke 4:29)

27. What was the Jewish traditional view of when the Christ would come? (John 7:27)

28. Christ was thought by some to be which three former prophets? (Matt. 16:14)

29. Who did Jesus say hath ascended up to heaven? (John 3:13)

30. Nicodemus defended Jesus in the council and was accused of being from where? (John 7:50, 52)

31. What entity recognized Jesus in the Synagogue at Capernaum? (Mark 1:23–24)

32. What was the first reaction of the wise men upon seeing the baby Jesus? (Matt. 2:11)

33. What did the multitude want to do with Jesus after the feeding of the five thousand? (John 6:15)

34. What was Jesus wrapped in at His birth? (Luke 2:7)

35. Jesus was put to death in the flesh, but quickened by the what? (1 Pet. 3:18)

36. What did Jesus say to the man who wanted to follow Him, but asked if he could bury his father first? (Matt. 8:21–22)

37. Jesus is the true vine, and what person is the husbandman? (John 15:1)

38. If you are ashamed of Jesus, who will be ashamed of you? (Mark 8:38)

39. Who gave Jesus his name? (Matt. 1:21–22)

40. According to John the Revelator, the testimony of Jesus is the spirit of what? (Rev. 19:10)

41. In the beginning, John states that the Word was with what person? (John 1:1)

42. Jesus purged our sins and became our what, with the Father? (Heb. 9:14–15)

43. Jesus first declared his Messiahship to whom? (John 4:7, 26)

44. Who were abiding in the fields at Jesus' birth? (Luke 2:8)

45. Because Jesus came eating and drinking they called Him a "winebibber" and what else? (Matt. 11:19)

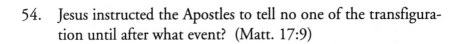

54. Jesus instructed the Apostles to tell no one of the transfiguration until after what event? (Matt. 17:9)

55. What are the names of the Apostles that were with Christ at the Transfiguration? (Matt. 17:1–2)

56. Which two ancient prophets appeared to Jesus at the Transfiguration? (Matt. 17:3)

57. What did Peter suggest building at the site of the Transfiguration? (Matt. 17:4)

58. What was identified as the site of the Transfiguration? (Matt. 17:1–2)

59. What was Peter, James and John's reaction to God's voice? (Matt. 17:6)

60. Who spoke to Peter, James, and John from heaven at the time of the Transfiguration? (Matt. 17:5)

61. What was the Father's voice projected from within at the Transfiguration? (Matt. 17:5)

62. What did the face of Christ shine like at the Transfiguration? (Matt. 17:2)

63. The leadership of the Jews asked Jesus, "If thou be _____, tell us plainly"? (John 10:24)

64. What was the question the Jews asked, because Jesus had never "learned"? (John 7:15)

65. Jesus asked, whence was John's baptism, "from Heaven or of man?" What was the Ruler's answer? (Matt. 21:25, 27)

66. Jesus was asked, "Is it lawful to give _____ unto Caesar, or not?" (Matt. 22:17)

67. What building sanctified the gold within it? (Matt. 23:17)

68. Who asked the question that precipitated Peter's third denial? (John 18:10, 26)

69. Who was Jesus referring to when He used the description. "A reed shaken in the wind?" (Matt. 11:7, 11)

70. Disciples of the Pharisees and Herodians came to Jesus and asked if it was lawful to pay tribute to what man? (Matt. 22:17)

71. What is the common name for the parable that came from the question, "Who is my neighbor?" (Luke 10:30–37)

72. What did the Sadducees question Jesus about, although they did not believe in it? (Matt. 22:23)

73. How many asked, "Master, is it I?" at the last supper? (Matt. 26:22, 25)

Solution on page 299

Across

4 In Matthew, the location of Christ's third temptation in the wilderness was on this high geological feature. (Matt. 4:8)

7 Jesus was tempted in the wilderness by this evil entity after his baptism. (Matt. 4:1)

8 According to Matthew, in his third temptation in the wilderness, the devil showed Jesus all the kingdoms of this orb. (Matt. 4:8)

11 According to James, God does not tempt this creation. (James 1:13)

12 In Jesus' answer to Satan's second temptation in the wilderness, Jesus said we should not do this to God. (Matt. 4:7)

13 Jesus fasted this number of days and nights before his temptations in the wilderness. (Matt. 4:2)

18 In the third temptation of Jesus in the wilderness (as recorded in Matthew), who did the devil want Jesus to fall down and worship? (Matt. 4:9)

19 In the first temptation in the wilderness, Satan challenged Jesus saying, "If thou be the Son of _____, command these stones be made bread." (Matt. 4:3)

20 Every man is tempted when he is

drawn away by these sinful desires. (James 1:14)

21 The members of this profession questioned Jesus tempting Him (plural). (Matt. 22:35)

Down

1 According to James, when lust hath conceived it brings forth this. (James 1:15)

2 James says to count it this happy emotion when we fall into temptation. (James 1:2)

3 In answer to the devil's first temptation, Jesus said that man does not live by this food staple alone. (Matt. 4:4)

5 Paul said that God has provided an escape for us when we are tempted beyond our _____(noun). (1 Cor. 10:13)

6 Jesus was led into the wilderness to be tempted of the devil by this member of the Godhead. (Matt. 4:1)

9 These heavenly beings came to Jesus after His temptations in the wilderness. (Matt. 4:11)

10 In reporting the order of Christ's temptations in the wilderness, Luke records Matthew's number three temptation as his number _____. (Luke 4:6, 9)

14 In the second temptation of Jesus in the wilderness, Matthew reports that Satan took the Savior to the pinnacle of this building. (Matt. 4:5)

15 As recorded in Matthew, to disguise his second temptation in the wilderness, the devil challenged Jesus to _____ Himself from the temple. (Matt. 4:6)

16 Paul declared that we should not let sin "reign in your mortal _____, that ye should obey it in the lusts thereof." (Rom. 6:12)

17 Paul taught that this physical part of man lusts against the Spirit. (Gal. 5:17)

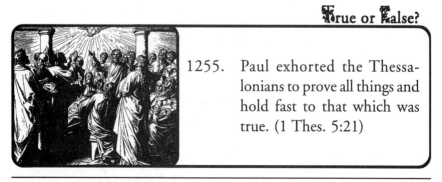

True or False?

1255. Paul exhorted the Thessalonians to prove all things and hold fast to that which was true. (1 Thes. 5:21)

74. What was the last thing the Apostles and Jesus did before leaving the location of the Last Supper? (Matt. 26:30)

75. What did Jesus gird Himself with at the Last Supper to wash the feet of the Apostles? (John 13:4)

76. At the Last Supper, the devil put it into the what of Judas, to betray the Lord? (John 13:2)

77. At the Last Supper, Jesus introduced what replacement for sacrifice? (Matt. 26:26–28)

78. At the Last Supper, Jesus washed the what, of the Apostles? (John 13:5)

    a. hands
    b. dishes
    c. feet

79. During the Last Supper, Philip asked Jesus to show the disciples what personage, and it would "sufficeth" them? (John 14:8)

80. After the Last Supper, Jesus was troubled in His what? (John 13:21)

81. What was the "new commandment" Jesus gave the Apostles at the Last Supper? (John 13:34)

82. At the Last Supper, Jesus said one of the Apostles would betray Him. With what question did the Apostles respond? (Matt. 26:22)

83. Jesus declared to his Apostles at the Last Supper that He was the what, the truth, and the life? (John 14:6)

84. The room for the Last Supper was located by the disciples by following a man who was bearing a pitcher of what? (Mark 14:13–14)

85. At the Last Supper, who asked Jesus, "how can we know the way"? (John 14:5)

86. At the Last Supper, Jesus said He would give what, to the Apostle who would betray Him? (John 13:26)

87. Jesus told his Apostles at the Last Supper that if we know Him, we should know who? (John 14:7)

Trick Question

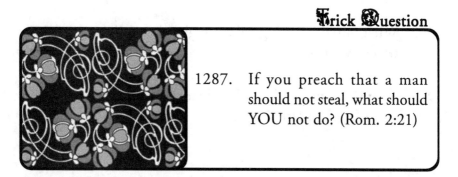

1287. If you preach that a man should not steal, what should YOU not do? (Rom. 2:21)

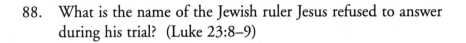

88. What is the name of the Jewish ruler Jesus refused to answer during his trial? (Luke 23:8–9)

89. What was the name of the high priest at the trial of Jesus? (Matt. 26:3)

90. According to John, Annas sent Christ bound to what person? (John 18:24)

91. What high priest commanded that Paul be smitten on the mouth? (Acts 23:2)

92. Finally, at Jesus' trial, how many false witnesses testified that Jesus said He would destroy the temple? (Matt. 26:60–61)

93. To what Roman official did the High Priest take Jesus to be tried? (Matt. 27:2)

94. What was the name of the King who also heard Paul's case after he was arrested, but before he went to Rome? (Acts 25:22–24)

95. What forbidden thing did the high priest do in anger at Jesus' trial? (Matt. 26:65)

96. After the guilty verdict, what three things did the Jewish court do to Jesus? (Matt. 26:67)

97. What was Jesus finally found guilty of at His trial before the Jewish leadership? (Matt. 26:65)

98. What part of Malchus' body did Peter strike with a sword at the arrest of Jesus? (John 18:10)

99. Which Apostle was with the band of men who came to arrest Jesus? (John 18:5)

100. What was the position of Caiaphas at the trial of Jesus? (Matt. 26:3)

101. The crown that was placed on Jesus' head by the soldiers was made of what? (Matt. 27:29)

102. At whose feet did the witnesses lay their clothes when they stoned Stephen? (Acts 7:58)

103. What is to be preached as a witness to all nations before the end shall come? (Matt. 24:14)

104. Paul said that in the mouth of two or three witnesses shall every what, be established? (2 Cor. 13:1)

105. John the Baptist was a witness to Christ, but Jesus said that an even greater witness was His what? (John 5:36)

106. Who are the two witnesses Jesus stated bore witness of His divinity? (John 8:18)

107. In John the Revelator's vision, how long will the two witnesses to the Jews lay dead in the streets of Jerusalem? (Rev. 11:9)

108. The two witnesses in Revelation 11 are referred to as two trees. What kind of trees? (Rev. 11:3–4)

109. What will kill the two witnesses to the Jews spoken of in Revelation, Chapter 11? (Rev. 11:7)

110. On the day of Pentecost, the Apostles declared they were witnesses of the what? (Acts 2:31–32)

111. John declares that what three bear witness in heaven? (1 John 5:7)

112. Saul was a witness to what disciple's death? (Acts 7:58–59)

113. John declares that what three things bear witness in the earth and agree as one? (1 John 5:8)

114. Jesus agreed that according to the rule of witnesses, if He only bore witness of Himself, it was what? (John 5:31)

True or False?

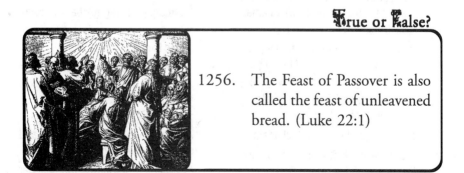

1256. The Feast of Passover is also called the feast of unleavened bread. (Luke 22:1)

JUDAS ISCARIOT
And The Word Was Made Flesh

Solution on page 284

```
T  H  I  R  T  Y  R  R  L  T  S
R  K  S  A  T  A  N  S  L  S  P
T  E  M  P  L  E  A  G  I  H  E
H  W  T  J  B  B  M  K  L  A  R
N  A  Q  H  A  A  A  G  M  S  D
T  M  N  S  I  S  G  A  H  U  I
Z  R  R  G  U  E  D  S  E  N  T
J  A  D  S  I  L  F  I  L  D  I
B  N  E  Z  E  N  T  M  E  E  O
H  J  W  C  J  K  G  O  F  R  N
N  R  A  W  K  H  R  N  T  K  M
```

- This is another name for the "field of blood" purchased by the betrayers' funds. (Acts 1:19)

- Judas betrayed the Lord for how many pieces of silver? (Matt. 26:15)

- Matthew says Judas Iscariot committed suicide by this method. (Matt. 27:5)

- This is what Judas did after receiving the sop from Jesus at the Last Supper. (John 13:30)

- Of the two appointed to fill Judas' position by the Apostles, one was named Matthias, and the other was named this. (Acts 1:23)

- After the sop was given to him, this evil entity entered Judas. (John 13:27)

- John tells us that Judas kept the money bag, and from the beginning was this. (John 12:6)

  (a) thief (b) beggar (c) charlatan

- Jesus called Judas, the Apostle He lost, a son of this. (John 17:12)

- This was the sign Judas gave to the arresting party when he identified and betrayed Christ. (Matt. 26:48)

- When Judas returned the thirty pieces of silver after Christ's trial, he cast them down in this building. (Matt. 27:3–5)

  (a) Pretorium
  (b) Chief Priest's house
  (c) Temple

- Judas was the treasurer for the Apostles and therefore, he kept this. (John 12:6)

  (a) money (b) bag (c) bank account

- This was the name of the father of Judas Iscariot. (John 13:2)

- This is the name of the person Luke states that Satan entered Judas to betray. (Luke 22:2–4)

- The book of Acts states that Judas Iscariot died by falling into a field and bursting this way. (Acts 1:18)

  (a) Open (b) Apart (c) Asunder

115. What is the name of the high priest's servant whose ear was cut off by Peter when Jesus was arrested? (John 18:10)

116. How many times did Jesus return to the sleeping Apostles in Gethsemane? (Matt. 26:40–45)

117. What is the name of the Garden where Jesus prayed before his betrayal? (Matt. 26:36)

118. Gethsemane was across what brook? (John 18:1)

119. What did Jesus ask to have pass from Him in Gethsemane? (Matt. 26:39)

120. What is the name of the Apostle who betrayed Jesus? (Matt. 26:14–15)

121. Which three Apostles went into Gethsemane with Jesus to pray? (Matt. 26:37; Matt. 4:21)

122. What were Peter, James, and John doing while Jesus prayed in Gethsemane? (Matt. 26:40)

123. As recorded in Matthew, what did the sign on Christ's cross read? (Matt. 27:37)

124. What came out of Jesus' side when it was pierced at the crucifixion? (John 19:34)

125. What does the word Golgotha mean? (Matt. 27:33)

126. What did they give to Jesus to drink at His crucifixion? (Matt. 27:34)

127. How many thieves were crucified with Christ? (Matt. 27:38)

128. What did Jesus do to the Roman guards that crucified Him? (Luke 23:34)

129. At the crucifixion, Jesus' coat was without what, so the soldiers gambled for it? (John 19:23–24)

130. What was the two word statement Jesus spoke from the cross? (John 19:28)

131. Who was compelled to carry Jesus' cross to the place of crucifixion? (Matt. 27:32)

132. Matthew records the names of three women who watched the crucifixion. What are their names? (Matt. 27:56)

133. What was the cry of Jesus on the cross as He gave up the ghost? (Luke 23:46)

134. What did Jesus "yield up" on the cross? (Matt. 27:50)

135. What was the color of the robe Jesus wore at His crucifixion? (Matt. 27:28)

136. What did one of the thieves ask of Jesus as He hung on the cross? (Luke 23:42)

137. What was "over all the land" from the crucifixion's sixth hour to the ninth hour? (Matt. 27:45)

138. What was Jesus' answer to the question of the thief on the cross? (Luke 23:43)

139. What is Matthew's name for the place of the crucifixion? (Matt. 27:33)

140. What did the soldiers place in Jesus' hand as they mocked Him prior to the crucifixion? (Matt. 27:29)

Trick Question

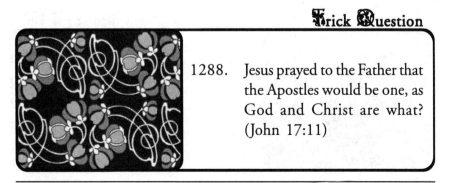

1288. Jesus prayed to the Father that the Apostles would be one, as God and Christ are what? (John 17:11)

141. How many days passed between the resurrection and the Ascension? (Acts 1:3)

142. How many angels (men in white apparel) stood by the Apostles at the Ascension? (Acts 1:10)

143. What is another name for the Mount of Ascension? (Acts 1:12)

144. What do the scriptures say is the distance from Jerusalem to the Ascension site on the Mount of Olives? (Acts 1:12)

145. What was the color of the clothing the angels wore at the Ascension? (Acts 1:10)

146. What received Jesus up into heaven at the Ascension? (Acts 1:9)

147. Who were commandments given through after the Ascension? (Acts 1:2)

True or False?

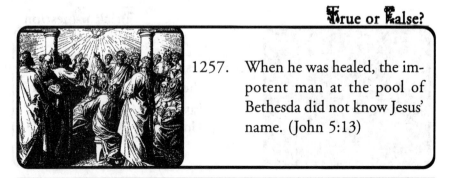

1257. When he was healed, the impotent man at the pool of Bethesda did not know Jesus' name. (John 5:13)

148. When Paul wrote to the Philippian Saints, he told them they were able to "_____ for his sake." (Philip. 1:29)

149. Paul said we suffer reproach because we trust in the living what? (1 Tim. 4:10)

150. The Thessalonian saints were suffering tribulations and what? (2 Thes. 1:4)

151. To Peter, it was better to suffer for "well doing" than for what? (1 Pet. 3:17)

152. According to Paul, though Jesus was a Son, what did He learn by the things He suffered? (Heb. 5:8)

153. According to Paul, what suffereth long and is kind? (1 Cor. 13:4)

Trick Question

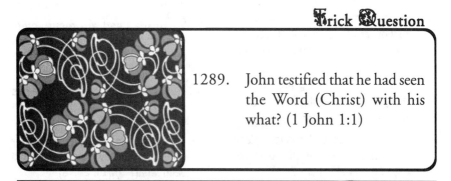

1289. John testified that he had seen the Word (Christ) with his what? (1 John 1:1)

RESURRECTION CROSSWORD
And The Word Was Made Flesh

Solution on page 293

Across

1 When Mary Magdalene saw Jesus at the sepulcher, she supposed Him to be this caretaker. (John 20:15)

4 This Jewish sect was grieved by the teaching of the Apostles that through Jesus came the resurrection of the dead. (Acts 4:1–2)

7 Matthew states that after the resurrection of Jesus, many graves did not remain closed, but were this. (Matt. 27:52–53)

8 Paul states that in the resurrection, there are both celestial and terrestrial types of what? (1 Cor. 15:40, 42)

10 The resurrection of Jesus took place on what the Jews designated as this day of the week. (Luke 24:1)

11 According to Paul, this is when the dead in Christ rise. (1 Thes. 4:16)

13 When the dead come forth, the good will be resurrected to this eternal state. (John 5:29)

14 How many Apostles and disciples were present to see the resurrected Jesus at the Sea of Tiberias? (John 21:2)

17 When the dead are resurrected, those that are evil come forth to the resurrection of this punishment. (John 5:29)

20 Paul said Christ was seen of this man, and then the Apostles after His resurrection. (1 Cor. 15:5)

21 The guards at Christ's sepulcher were bribed to say that His body had been what? (Matt. 28:13)

22 Jesus stated that His resurrected body was made of bones and this. (Luke 24:39)

Down

2 This was the first word Mary Magdalene used when she addressed the resurrected Christ. (John 20:16)

3 The Apostles thought that the report of the women that Jesus had risen was as these idle stories. (Luke 24:11)

4 After the resurrection, Jesus instructed Thomas to touch the nail prints in His hands, to thrust his hand into this, and be believing. (John 20:27)

5 Our preaching and our faith is in vain if this person is not risen. (1 Cor. 15:14)

6 After the resurrection, this was the number of days between the first and second visits of Jesus to the Apostles. (John 20:26)

9 The Apostles thought Jesus was this part of the soul when He first appeared to them in the upper room after the resurrection. (Luke 24:37)

10 In which chapter of 1 Corinthians does Paul argue in favor of the resurrection?

11 To worship the resurrected Jesus, the women took hold of these. (Matt. 28:9)

12 On the morning of the resurrection, there was an earthquake, and an angel removed this hard object from Christ's tomb. (Matt. 28:2)

15 After the resurrection, Jesus appeared to two men as they traveled on the road to this city. (Luke 24:13)

16 When he entered Christ's sepulcher, Peter saw the linen clothes that had covered the Savior and this facial burial covering. (John 20:6–7)

18 Mary Magdalene saw two of these inside the sepulcher. (John 20:12)

19 After the resurrection, Jesus was seen of this person last of all, as one born out of due time. (1 Cor. 15:8)

True or False?

1258. After Jesus left Nazareth for the ministry, He dwelt in Nain. (Matt. 4:13)

THE SECOND COMING
And The Word Was Made Flesh

Solution on page 295

```
L  I  G  H  T  E  N  I  N  G  S  P  K  K  M
W  A  T  C  H  N  B  S  N  E  T  R  J  M  L
Z  K  M  Y  J  Y  O  L  K  Q  B  O  R  A  P
H  C  V  E  N  G  E  A  N  C  E  P  R  R  F
X  E  R  M  N  T  U  N  H  G  S  H  R  R  A
L  N  A  M  L  Q  F  D  Z  R  S  E  S  I  L
L  M  M  V  H  K  H  S  E  W  H  T  R  A  L
Z  H  T  T  E  N  V  D  O  R  N  S  G  G  I
Y  N  R  Q  I  N  N  R  E  E  Z  M  D  E  N
Q  A  O  S  N  O  R  H  M  B  B  R  L  V  G
E  J  Z  I  W  O  T  E  M  M  U  N  M  N  A
W  G  W  R  S  A  L  P  D  W  H  R  R  R  W
R  W  M  H  F  E  D  J  G  Q  R  E  N  L  A
P  C  A  U  G  H  T  U  P  Z  Z  F  A  E  Y
T  H  I  N  G  S  D  X  B  R  B  Z  N  T  D
```

- The disasters predicted before the Second Coming are said to be but the beginning of these. (Matt. 24:8)

- The purpose of Elias coming before Christ's Second Coming is to restore all what? (Matt. 17:11)

  (a) doctrines
  (b) authority
  (c) things

- In the day of the Lord, the earth and all works therein shall be this. (2 Pet. 3:10)

  (a) burned
  (b) destroyed
  (c) broken up

- Before the flood came at the time of Noah, all were eating, drinking, and giving in this. (Matt. 24:38)

- These will occur in diverse places around the earth before the Lord's coming. (Matt. 24:7)

- Jesus described His coming like this comes out of the east and moves to the west. (Matt. 24:27)
  - (a) wind
  - (b) sun
  - (c) lightning

- In the day of the Lord, we look for a new earth and a new this (singular). (2 Pet. 3:13)

- These land masses will flee away during the last earthquake before the Second Coming. (Rev. 16:20)

- The man of this will be revealed before the Lord comes. (2 Thes. 2:3)
  - (a) evil
  - (b) sin
  - (c) temptation

- Paul taught that those righteous still alive when Christ comes shall be this with Him. (1 Thes. 4:17)
  - (a) caught up
  - (b) destroyed
  - (c) transfigured

- In the day of the Lord, the elements shall melt with fervent what? (2 Pet. 3:10)

- Paul taught that before the Second Coming there would be this, and the man of sin would be revealed. (2 Thes. 2:3)

- The only person who knows the day and hour of Christ's Second Coming is who? (Matt. 24:36)
  - (a) Holy Ghost
  - (b) Son
  - (c) Father

- Many of these false ones shall arise and deceive many before the Lord comes. (Matt. 24:11)

- Because we do not know the time of His coming, we should always be alert and do this for the coming of the Son of Man. (Mark 13:37)
  - (a) watch
  - (b) look
  - (c) be available

- Peter states that when the Lord comes, the heavens will pass away with a great what? (2 Pet. 3:10)
  - (a) heat
  - (b) noise
  - (c) wreckage

- Before the Lord comes, great signs and these are shown by false Christs and false prophets. (Matt. 24:24)

- Paul declares that when the Lord comes, He will take this type of revenge on those who know not God. (2 Thes. 1:8)

- Peter declares that these will melt with a fervent heat at the Second Coming. (2 Pet. 3:10)

- Jesus prophesied that it will be like the days of this ancient prophet before the Second Coming (common spelling). (Matt. 24:37)

Who Are The Players?

154. What was Jesus' answer to Mary's question in the temple at age twelve? (Luke 2:49)

155. What was the marital status of Mary when she was "found with child"? (Matt. 1:18)

156. What was offered in the temple for Mary's cleansing as a result of Jesus' birth? (Luke 2:24)

157. What was the name of the angel that appeared to Mary (the Lord's mother), announcing the coming birth of Jesus? (Luke 1:26–27)

158. Who was the husband of Mary (mother of Jesus)? (Matt. 1:16)

159. What was the "title" Jesus gave his mother when He addressed her from the cross? (John 19:26)

160. Matthew describes Mary as being with child of whom? (Matt. 1:18)

ABOUT PEOPLE
Who Are The Players?

Solution on page 273

```
L  J  N  W  M  Q  R  M  R  R  G  Q  T  K  C  W  R  D
X  N  N  H  O  H  V  J  B  I  F  O  B  E  Y  E  D  M
K  T  N  T  L  R  L  L  O  C  K  X  F  T  M  X  R  R
L  P  B  O  R  T  T  X  T  H  M  F  S  L  P  W  S  R
K  N  R  N  N  R  F  H  W  H  N  O  C  Z  S  N  Y  D
R  P  N  A  R  E  Z  X  Y  M  H  O  T  U  A  N  Y  D
H  L  P  Y  Y  L  N  K  G  G  L  D  I  T  V  C  C  S
C  A  N  D  A  C  E  G  Y  Q  G  R  I  N  J  M  E  N
T  G  B  N  K  F  L  L  R  X  T  R  N  N  V  I  B  F
Y  U  W  K  S  L  O  D  S  E  A  N  H  T  D  L  V  P
M  E  O  T  P  H  Z  E  M  M  E  D  G  O  B  Q  M  V
X  S  M  M  I  M  I  E  A  K  E  B  V  H  O  G  Y
V  T  A  W  R  T  D  S  K  K  P  Y  W  M  D  M  X  P
R  R  N  L  I  N  V  X  U  R  S  B  M  S  K  R  W  P
W  N  Z  N  T  Z  N  B  N  U  D  K  I  J  E  W  S  P
M  R  G  P  S  G  E  R  B  B  N  W  M  R  K  K  N  B
Q  I  Z  F  P  R  T  W  R  W  C  T  L  E  A  V  E  W
D  T  S  H  E  P  H  E  R  D  M  I  R  A  C  L  E  S
```

- This fell upon Cornelius and all his house as Peter preached to them. (Acts 10:44)

- This was the name of the Queen of Ethiopia as recorded in Acts. (Acts 8:27)

  (a) Sheba
  (b) Candace
  (c) Tabitha

- This was Mark's (companion to Paul and Barnabus) first name. (Acts 15:37)

- The people marveled that even these unclean, disembodied entities obeyed Jesus. (Mark 1:27)

- Disorderly, nonworking people were called what by Paul? (2 Thes. 3:11)

- Jesus observed that the multitudes were as sheep, not having one of these. (Matt. 9:36)

- The centurion who asked Jesus to heal his servant would not allow Jesus into his home because he said he was not this. (Matt. 8:8)

- The people sought Jesus after the feeding of the five thousand because this was free. (John 6:26)
  - (a) time
  - (b) blessings
  - (c) food

- Paul declared that the Greeks always sought after this. (1 Cor. 1:22)
  - (a) philosophy
  - (b) wisdom
  - (c) knowledge

- The multitude followed Jesus *before* the feeding of the five thousand because they had seen these. (John 6:2)
  - (a) wonders
  - (b) miracles
  - (c) disciples

- This was the nationality of the men who asked the Apostle Philip to speak with Jesus. (John 12:20)

- Jesus said that men who were this would hardly be able to enter the kingdom. (Matt. 19:23)

- The Jews accused Christ of being from this hated race (plural). (John 8:48)

- After healing the possessed man in the land of the Gadarene and the destruction of their swine, the people asked Jesus to do this. (Matt. 8:34)
  - (a) stay
  - (b) teach
  - (c) leave

- The Sermon on the Mount tells us that we should do this for the people who despitefully use us. (Matt. 5:44)

- Was the Samaritan that Jesus spoke with by the well a man or a woman? (John 4:7)

- Peter said self-willed people are not afraid to speak evil of these. (2 Pet. 2:10)
  - (a) leaders
  - (b) rulers
  - (c) dignities

- Had the Philippians always obeyed or disobeyed the gospel? (Philip. 2:12)

- How many people did Paul declare were righteous? (Rom. 3:10)

- When the blind men of Jericho called after Jesus, the people did this to them. (Matt. 20:31)

- Mark said the people who pressed to touch the hem of Jesus' garment were diseased with all manner of these. (Mark 3:10)

- This man caused an uproar in Ephesus over the goddess Diana. (Acts 19:24)

- John said that some at Smyrna claimed to be of this nationality and were not. (Rev. 2:9)

161. Joseph (Mary's husband) received his revelations from God by what method? (Matt. 2:19)

162. Who told Joseph to take Mary to wife? (Matt. 1:20)

163. What was the reason Joseph and Mary went to Bethlehem before Christ's birth? (Luke 2:3–4)

164. What was the occupation of Joseph, husband of Mary? (Matt. 13:55)

165. Joseph (Mary's husband) is described as what type of man? (Matt. 1:19)

166. Who told Joseph to take Jesus to Egypt? (Matt. 2:13)

167. What was Joseph's initial reaction when he discovered Mary was with child? (Matt. 1:19)

168. Who was the wife of Joseph (the stepfather of Jesus)? (Matt. 1:16)

169. What city did Joseph go to when he returned from Egypt with Mary and the baby Jesus? (Matt. 2:23)

183.
Who was sitting in a tree to see Jesus because he was small of stature?
(Luke 19:2–5)

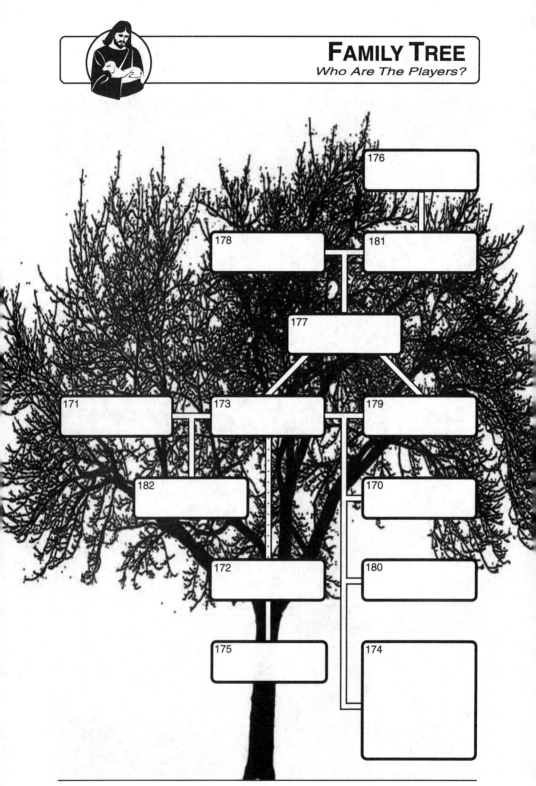

176

178

181

177

171

173

179

182

170

172

180

175

174

170. When Jesus taught in His own country, the people questioned His claims because they knew His mother, brothers, and who? (Matt. 13:56)

171. Who did Jesus claim was His father? (John 5:18)

172. What relative did Mary immediately visit after her conception? (Luke 1:40)

173. Who was the mother of Jesus? (Matt. 1:16)

174. James is singularly named as one of the Lord's brothers (Gal 1:19). What are the names of the other three named brothers of Jesus? (Matt. 13:55)

175. Zacharias was struck dumb as a sign, he spoke again at the naming of whom? (Luke 1:63–64)

176. Jesus was from which tribe in Israel? (Matt. 1:2–3)

177. From which king of Judah was Jesus a descendant? (Matt. 1:6)

178. Who was the ancestor of Christ that was a Moabitess damsel? (Matt. 1:5)

179. Who is the stepfather of Jesus? (Matt. 1:16)

180. Paul met with which brother of the Lord? (Gal. 1:19)

181. Which of Jesus' ancestors was of the tribe of Judah and married Ruth? (Matt. 1:5)

182. Who was the first born son of Mary? (Matt. 1:16)

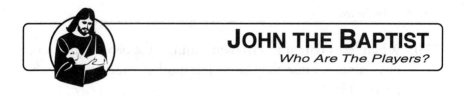
Solution on page 283

Across

2 Both the disciples of John the Baptist and the disciples of Jesus performed this ordinance. (John 3:22–23)

4 The rulers of the Jews said John the Baptist had a devil because he did not eat or drink this normal fare. (Matt. 11:18)

7 Who asked John the Baptist if he was the Christ, the Pharisees or the Sadducees? (John 1:24)

10 The daughter of Herodias requested that John the Baptist's head be brought to her in this container. (Matt. 14:8)

11 John the Baptist said that he was not the bridegroom, but a _____ of the bridegroom. (John 3:29)

12 This brother of Peter was a disciple of John the Baptist before he followed Jesus. (John 1:40)

14 To verify Himself to the disciples of John the Baptist, Jesus performed several of these. (Matt. 11:4–5)

15 Jesus said He that was this in the kingdom of heaven, was greater than John the Baptist. (Matt. 11:11)

17 John the Baptist said he was unworthy to bear this footwear of Jesus? (Matt. 3:11)

18 John the Baptist was confined in this when he sent two of his disciples to ask if Jesus was the Messiah. (Matt. 11:2)

20 The woman who danced and asked for the head of John the Baptist was

what relation of Herodias? (Matt. 14:6)

22 John records that when Jesus approached John the Baptist, the Baptist called Him the _____ of God. (John 1:29)

23 John the Baptist, until the day he was shown unto Israel, lived in these arid places. (Luke 1:80)

24 John the Baptist came out of the wilderness preaching that the kingdom of heaven was at hand and exhorting people to do this. (Matt. 3:2)

Down

1 This is the name of John the Baptist's father. (Luke 1:13)

3 John the Baptist baptized in this river. (Matt. 3:5–6)

5 John the Baptist said that Jesus must increase while he must do this. (John 3:30)

6 John the Baptist said that after his baptism with water would come one who would baptize with the Holy Ghost and this. (Matt. 3:11)

8 John the Baptist said God could raise up children of Abraham from these hard objects. (Matt. 3:9)

9 This is the manner in which John the Baptist was put to death. (Matt. 14:10)

13 This is the name of John the Baptist's mother. (Luke 1:13)

16 John the Baptist was to come in the spirit and power of this ancient prophet. (Luke 1:13, 17)

19 John the Baptist's clothing was made of the hair of this animal. (Matt. 3:4)

21 The law and the prophets were preached until the time of John the Baptist. Since that time the kingdom of this Deity has been preached. (Luke 16:16)

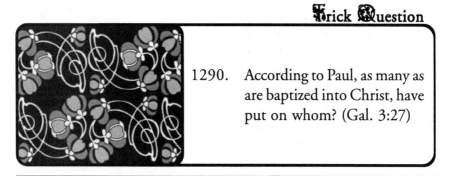

Trick Question

1290. According to Paul, as many as are baptized into Christ, have put on whom? (Gal. 3:27)

PETER MATCH GAME
Who Are The Players?

Match the questions on the left with the answers on the right.
The solution is on page 292.

A. Jesus healed the mother of Peter's wife of this malady. (Matt. 8:14–15)

Patience

B. Peter's death was foreshadowed as this type. (John 21:18)

Barjona

C. Peter taught that we also should have a more sure word of this. (2 Pet. 1:19)

Wept

D. This is the name of the man Peter healed of the palsy. (Acts 9:34)

A fever

E. Peter went out and did this after he had denied knowing the Lord three times. (Matt. 26:75)

God

F. Peter envisioned this object that was knitted together at the four corners. (Acts 10:11)

Aeneas

G. Peter said we should add this to our temperance. (2 Pet. 1:6)

Go fishing

H. Peter said Paul's writings were sometimes _____ to understand. (2 Pet. 3:16)

Satan

I. While waiting for the resurrected Jesus in Galilee, Peter decided to do this. (John 21:1–3)

Hard

J. Peter told the council that the Apostles ought to obey this Deity, rather than men. (Acts 5:29)

Prophecy

K. Jesus said this evil person desired to have Peter and to sift him as wheat. (Luke 22:31)

A sheet

L. This was Peter's surname. (Matt. 16:17)

Crucifixion

184. Peter said we should add to our godliness what? (2 Pet. 1:7)

185. Paul abode with Peter how many days when he first returned to Jerusalem? (Gal. 1:18)

186. Who did Jesus state had revealed His divinity to Peter? (Matt. 16:17)

187. What was Peter's answer when asked the question: "Men and brethren, what shall we do?" (Acts 2:37–38)

188. Peter asked the Lord that not only his feet be washed, but what else? (John 13:9)

189. Who did the people bring into the streets, hoping the shadow of Peter's passing might "overshadow" some of them? (Acts 5:15)

190. Peter states that it is better to have not known the way at all, than to know it and then what? (2 Pet. 2:21)

191. Peter was accused of eating with what type of unclean person? (Acts 11:3)

192. Jesus referred to Peter as "Satan" because he did what? (Matt. 16:22–23)

193. When the Apostles saw Jesus walking on water, what did Peter ask? (Matt. 14:28)

194. What city did John the Revelator see coming down from heaven adorned as a bride? (Rev. 21:2)

195. In John's vision, how many seals sealed the little book? (Rev. 5:1)

196. Who had the seven last plagues filled with the wrath of God in John the Revelator's vision? (Rev. 15:1)

197. At the opening of the seventh seal in John the Revelator's vision, there is silence in heaven. How long will it last? (Rev. 8:1)

198. In John the Revelator's vision, why did the merchants weep and mourn at the destruction of the great symbolic city? (Rev. 18:11)

199. In John the Revelator's vision, the Lord was not pleased with the church at Thyatira because they ate what things? (Rev. 2:20)

200. In the sixth of the last seven plagues in John's vision, what river is dried up? (Rev. 16:12)

201. In John the Revelator's vision, how long was the woman nourished in the wilderness? (Rev. 12:14)

202. John received his Revelation while he was in the Spirit on what day? (Rev. 1:10)

203. In John the Revelator's vision, which angel loosed the four angels that were bound in the river Euphrates? (Rev. 9:14)

204. Generally speaking, John the Revelator addressed the Book of Revelation to the seven what, which were in Asia? (Rev. 1:4)

205. In John the Revelator's vision, when the heavenly temple of God was opened, what "testament" did he see? (Rev. 11:19)

206. In John the Revelator's vision, who could open the seals of the little book? (Rev. 5:5)

207. In John the Revelator's vision, what is the second of the last seven plagues? (Rev. 16:3)

208. What did the good woman "clothed with the sun," have on her head in John's vision? (Rev. 12:1)

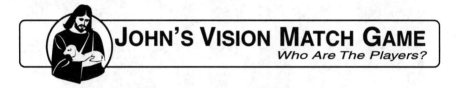

JOHN'S VISION MATCH GAME
Who Are The Players?

Match the questions on the left with the answers on the right.
The solution is on page 284.

A. At Ephesus, some claimed to be these religious agents, but were not. (Rev. 2:2)	Seven
B. The evil woman in John's vision represented one of these metropolitan entities.(Rev. 17:18)	Waters
C. The little book eaten by John tasted like this in his mouth. (Rev. 10:10)	A city
D. The beast of the sea John saw in his vision had this many heads. (Rev. 13:1)	Heaven
E. The devil's armies will eventually gather here to battle God. (Rev. 16:16)	Honey
F. The two witnesses of Revelation, have the power to "shut" this. (Rev. 11:6)	Armageddon
G. An angel told John to do this with a little book. (Rev. 10:9)	Eat it
H. The voice of Jesus was as the sound of many of these. (Rev. 1:15)	Apostles

Solution on page 293

Across

2 In John the Revelator's vision, how many beasts did he see at the throne of God? (Rev. 4:6)

3 Regarding the four beasts of John the Revelator's vision: this one looked like the face of what Homo Sapiens? (Rev. 4:7)

4 In John the Revelator's vision, the evil woman is drunken with the life-giving substance that runs through your veins. (Rev. 17:6)

6 Regarding the four beasts of John the Revelator's vision: this one looked like what flying symbol of the USA? (Rev. 4:7)

7 In John's vision, the seventh of the last seven plagues included what we call these great flashes in the sky during storms. (Rev. 16: 17–18)

8 In John the Revelator's vision, the second evil beast deceived men by performing what acts? (Rev. 13:14)

12 John the Revelator saw the throne of God, and around it—like an emerald—was what multicolored arch? (Rev. 4:3)

14 Regarding the four beasts of John

the Revelator's vision: this one looked like what the offspring of a cow is called. (Rev. 4:7)

15 In John the Revelator's vision, the censer cast to earth by an angel was filled with fire from what temple sacrificial pedestal? (Rev. 8:5)

16 In John the Revelator's vision, how many wings did each beast have? (Rev. 4:8)

18 In John the Revelator's vision, the fourth of the last seven plagues is scorching with fire and what else? (Rev. 16:8–9)

19 Is the death John the Revelator describes as a lake of fire and brimstone the first death or the second death? (Rev. 20:14)

20 In John the Revelator's vision, how many churches did the candlesticks represent? (Rev. 1:20)

22 In John the Revelator's vision, what sharp, two-edged instrument went out of Jesus' mouth? (Rev. 1:16)

24 In John's vision, the horse that had power to take peace from the earth was what color? (Rev 6:4)

27 In the third of the last seven plagues in John's vision, what became like blood? (Rev. 16:4)

29 John the Revelator taught that God would "spue" you out of His mouth if you were neither hot nor cold, but in what state of devotion? (Rev. 3:16)

30 In John's vision, the horse that went forth conquering was what color? (Rev. 6:2)

31 In John the Revelator's vision, the fourth of the last seven plagues is scorching with what element and heat? (Rev. 16:8–9)

32 In John the Revelator's vision, the ten horns of the beast represented ten what? (Rev. 17:12)

33 In John the Revelator's vision, what falls from heaven during the last plague to destroy the crops of the earth? (Rev. 16:21)

35 In John the Revelator's vision, how many horns did the beast of the sea have? (Rev. 13:1)

36 In John the Revelator's vision, the golden vials were full of odors, which is interpreted as what utterances of the saints? (Rev. 5:8)

37 In John the Revelator's vision, the locusts were shaped like what animal? (Rev. 9:7)

38 In John the Revelator's vision of Jesus, the Lord's feet were described as like what fine polished metal? (Rev. 1:15)

Down

1 In John's vision, the seventh of the last seven plagues included what we call the shaking of the earth. (Rev. 16: 17–18)

2 In John the Revelator's vision of Jesus, Jesus' eyes were like this element of fire. (Rev. 1:14)

5 In John the Revelator's vision, the fifth of the last seven plagues is what occurs when the sun goes down. (Rev. 16:10)

9 In John the Revelator's vision, the angel reaped the earth with a what? (Rev. 14:14–15)

10 In John the Revelator's vision, what is the first of the last seven plagues (plural)? (Rev. 16:2)

11 In John's vision, the horse that went

forth with a pair of balances in his hand was what color? (Rev 6:5)

13 In John the Revelator's vision, the king over the locusts is called what in Hebrew? (Rev. 9:11)

17 In John the Revelator's vision, the beast from the sea was like what animal? (Rev. 13:1–2)

20 In John the Revelator's vision, the countenance of Jesus was as brilliant as what orb? (Rev. 1:16)

21 John the Revelator said, he that overcomes shall not have his name blotted from this tome of life. (Rev. 3:5)

22 In John the Revelator's vision, the locusts that came out of the smoke were given power like what stinging creatures? (Rev. 9:3)

23 In John the Revelator's vision, the beast with seven heads and ten horns was given his power by what mythical "giant lizard"? (Rev. 13:2)

25 In John the Revelator's vision, the great dragon represents what evil personage? (Rev. 12:9)

26 In John's vision, the horse whose name was death and hell was what color? (Rev. 6:8)

28 In John's vision, the seventh of the last seven plagues included what we call these great noises during storms. (Rev. 16: 17–18)

30 John the Revelator said he that overcomes shall be clothed in what color raiment? (Rev. 3:5)

34 Regarding the four beasts of John the Revelator's vision: this one looked like what they call the king of beasts. (Rev. 4:7)

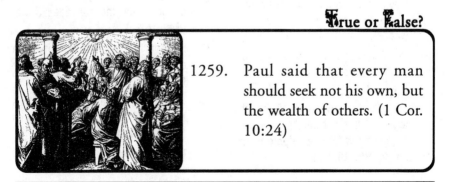

True or False?

1259. Paul said that every man should seek not his own, but the wealth of others. (1 Cor. 10:24)

209. Paul tells us that from a child, Timothy knew what holy records? (2 Tim. 3:15)

210. What did Paul require of Timothy because of the Jews? (Acts 16:1, 3)

211. Paul admonished Timothy to not neglect the what, that was in him? (1 Tim. 4:14)

212. Paul charges Timothy to not give heed to fables and endless what? (1 Tim. 1:4)

213. Paul calls Timothy what family relation? (1 Tim. 1:2)

214. Paul said that Timothy was to shun profane and vain what? (2 Tim. 2:16)

215. Paul, while giving Timothy many requirements, begins by stating that Bishops must be what? (1 Tim. 3:2)

216. Paul warned Timothy that people might despise him because of his what? (1 Tim. 4:12)

217. Timothy was told not to give heed to endless genealogies and what type of stories? (1 Tim. 1:4)

PAUL WORD SEARCH
Who Are The Players?

Solution on page 292

```
D  M  B  S  D  B  A  P  T  I  S  M  C  Q  R  C
T  J  F  L  I  P  H  A  R  I  S  E  E  R  M  R
P  R  Q  I  J  N  R  Y  K  Q  L  N  E  Z  P  S
R  N  S  B  G  E  N  K  L  P  K  K  K  A  J  A
A  T  M  H  P  H  M  E  M  J  A  Z  T  F  V  T
N  F  P  I  I  T  T  A  R  M  R  I  X  B  N  A
A  D  V  Q  B  P  X  J  T  S  L  M  M  E  T  N
N  A  T  T  O  E  W  N  G  E  G  M  T  G  H  L
I  B  G  N  N  K  E  R  M  X  Q  N  N  H  R  L
A  Z  R  R  D  T  K  N  E  J  O  I  D  J  E  C
S  A  P  O  S  T  L  E  W  C  N  A  X  R  E  H
G  O  D  F  O  R  B  I  D  R  K  H  J  K  R  A
B  Q  N  R  N  T  H  Z  A  N  X  K  E  E  Y  R
J  T  R  F  K  W  Y  E  T  V  P  M  M  A  W  I
X  R  Q  T  R  P  L  M  H  G  L  Q  C  R  D  T
R  O  M  A  N  S  C  O  U  R  G  I  N  G  H  Y
```

- Paul said that whatsoever state he was in, he had learned to be this. (Philip. 4:11)

- What is the two-word answer Paul uses when he poses an obviously contradictory question about God or His doctrine? (Rom. 11:1)

  (a) God forbid
  (b) God help
  (c) God forgive

- As he was about to die, Paul declared to Timothy that he had fought a good what? (2 Tim. 4:7)

- This is the number of days that Saul waited in Damascus fasting and without sight, before he was healed. (Acts 9:9)

  (a) two
  (b) three
  (c) four

- Festus told Paul that too much of this had made him mad. (Acts 26:24)

  (a) education
  (b) research
  (c) learning

- Before Paul declared that he was a

Roman citizen, a guard ordered him punished by this means. (Acts 22:25)

- On his way to Rome from his trial, Paul's ship was delayed because of this. (Acts 27:41)

  (a) shipwreck
  (b) wind
  (c) storm

- While in Damascus, Saul saw a vision of this man coming to heal him. (Acts 9:12)

- This is the name of the island located close to the place where Paul was shipwrecked. (Acts 28:1)

  (a) Crete
  (b) Melita
  (c) Malta

- Paul declared that he had been called to this office in the ministry. (Rom. 1:1)

- Paul shaved this in Cenchrea to visually express his vow. (Acts 18:18)

  (a) beard
  (b) head
  (c) chest

- Paul said that this person had hindered him from going to the Thessalonians. (1 Thes. 2:18)

  (a) God
  (b) Satan
  (c) Peter

- This was Paul's occupation. (Acts 18:1, 3)

- The magistrates feared Paul when they discovered he was this citizenship. (Acts 16:38)

  (a) Jewish
  (b) Greek
  (c) Roman

- Paul declared himself to be the chief of these. (1 Tim. 1:15)

  (a) Apostles
  (b) servants
  (c) sinners

- Writing to the Philippians from Rome, Paul said he was in these restraints. (Philip. 1:13)

- Paul said he had properly set a good this before the Philippians. (Philip. 4:9)

  (a) beginning
  (b) help
  (c) example

- Paul said he was sent by the Lord not to perform this ordinance, but to preach the gospel. (1 Cor. 1:17)

- To preach Christ to the Jews, Paul became this. (1 Cor. 9:20)

  (a) a Jew
  (b) a priest
  (c) a Pharisee

- Paul said that though he had all knowledge and all faith, he was nothing without this. (1 Cor. 13:2)

- Paul was bitten by one of these on the island after the shipwreck. (Acts 28:3)

  (a) a snake
  (b) a baboon
  (c) a viper

- Paul was a member of this strict Jewish religious sect before his conversion to Christ. (Acts 23:6)

218. What did the Jews counsel to do with Saul after his conversion to Christ? (Acts 9:23)

219. What was Saul let down in from the walls of Damascus to save his life? (Acts 9:25)

220. Saul was taught at the feet of what teacher? (Acts 22:3)

221. Paul, as Saul, persecuted the church and did what, to it? (Gal. 1:13)

222. What is the name of the Jewish Sorcerer found by Saul at Paphos? (Acts 13:6)

223. Who appeared to Saul on the road to Damascus? (Acts 9:5)

224. Who introduced Saul to the Apostles at Jerusalem? (Acts 9:27)

225. What was the first thing that happened to Saul after he received a vision on the road to Damascus? (Acts 9:8)

226. What did Saul do in Damascus while he was blind? (Acts 9:9)

227. What did God tell Ananias would happen to Saul after Saul's conversion for His name's sake? (Acts 9:16)

228. How long was Paul "in the deep" as the result of a shipwreck? (2 Cor. 11:25)

229. What caused Paul to stop at the island of Melita on his way to Rome? (Acts 27:41–44; 28:1)

230. If Paul did not preach willingly, what did he say was committed to him? (1 Cor. 9:17)

231. What did the people of Iconium do to Paul? (Acts 14:19)

232. Paul said he knew a man who had been caught up to which heaven? (2 Cor. 12:2)

233. Paul said he suffered shipwreck how many times? (2 Cor. 11:25)

234. According to Paul, by what faculty did Abel offer to God a more excellent sacrifice? (Heb. 11:4)

235. Paul stated that his "thorn in the flesh," was a messenger from whom, to buffet him? (2 Cor. 12:7)

236. Paul was born to (did not purchase) what citizenship? (Acts 22:27–29)

237. Paul performed healing miracles by sending what personal clothing items from his body to complete the healing? (Acts 19:12)

238. Had Paul not done what, he might have been freed by Agrippa? (Acts 26:32)

239. Paul said he gave no offence so that what, would be not blamed? (2 Cor. 6:3)

240. The Jews of Thessalonica accused Paul and Jason of turning the world what way, because of their teaching? (Acts 17:6)

241. Dissension between Paul and Barnabus over whom, caused their separation? (Acts 15:37, 39)

242. Paul was beaten in Thyatira for performing what miracle? (Acts 16:16, 18, 23)

243. What was the unrealistic vow taken by certain Jews, until they killed Paul? (Acts 23:12)

244. Paul said he had been beaten with rods how many times? (2 Cor. 11:25)

245. Paul boldly stated that he was not ashamed of what? (Rom. 1:16)

246. Paul declared in Philippians that he was in a strait betwixt what two? (Philip. 1:22–23)

247. What bodily "things" did Paul say could not inherit the kingdom of God? (1 Cor. 15:50)

248. What did the chief priests want to do with Lazarus after he was raised from the dead? (John 12:10)

249. Because they had misunderstood Him, Jesus told the Apostles plainly that Lazarus was what? (John 11:14)

250. How long did Jesus wait after hearing that Lazarus was sick before returning to Bethany? (John 11:6)

251. After the raising of Lazarus, what High Priest said that one man should die for the people? (John 11:49–50)

252. The body of Lazarus was bound hand and foot in what? (John 11:44)

253. Jesus said the sickness of Lazarus was for what purpose? (John 11:4)

254. When Lazarus came forth from the tomb, his face was bound with what? (John 11:44)

255. In the parable of Lazarus and the rich man, who did the rich man want sent to his five brothers? (Luke 16:30)

256. In the parable of Lazarus and the rich man, where did Lazarus go after death? (Luke 16:22)

257. In the parable of Lazarus and the rich man, Lazarus was full of what? (Luke 16:20)

258. What did the Pharisees take council to do to Jesus after the raising of Lazarus? (John 11:53–54)

259. In the parable of Lazarus and the rich man, what licked Lazarus' sores? (Luke 16:21)

260. When Jesus said He would go to Lazarus, which Apostle said he would go and die with Him? (John 11:16)

261. Who sent the message to Jesus that Lazarus was sick? (John 11:3)

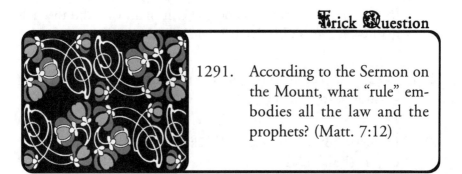

Trick Question

1291. According to the Sermon on the Mount, what "rule" embodies all the law and the prophets? (Matt. 7:12)

MEN MATCH GAME #1

Match the questions on the left with the answers on the right.
The solution is on page 288.

A. According to James, a perfect man offends not in this. (James 3:2)

Theophilus

B. A person has no greater what, than to lay down his life for friends? (John 15:13)

Lawless

C. Paul said that a man should be ashamed if he wore this long. (1 Cor. 11:14)

Burden

D. The Gospel of Luke was written to this person. (Luke 1:3)

Prayer

E. Paul states that every man should bear his own what? (Gal. 6:5)

Blindness

F. Jesus healed a man born with this malady. (John 9:1)

Word

G. Paul said the law was not for the righteous, but for the person that was this. (1 Tim. 1:9)

The Law

H. Paul taught that the man is not without this person in the Lord. (1 Cor. 11:11)

Woman

I. This avails much, if it is done fervently by a righteous man. (James 5:16)

Hair

J. Paul taught that no man is justified by this. (Gal. 3:11)

Love

Challenged by the New Testament

Solution on page 300

Across

1 This woman attended to Paul and Silas in Thyatira. (Acts 16:14)

3 When Jesus told the Samaritan woman about her _____, she perceived that He was a prophet. (John 4:18–19)

5 This was the first sister to go to Jesus when He returned to Bethany for the raising of Lazarus. (John 11:20)

9 Paul said that young widows who go from house to house are tattlers and these types of gossips. (1 Tim. 5:13)

10 This is the name of the sister of Martha and Lazarus. (Luke 10:39)

14 After speaking with Jesus, the Samaritan woman went into the city leaving this container by the well. (John 4:28)

15 Paul taught that the wives of deacons should be grave and not this type of gossipers. (1 Tim. 3:11)

17 Paul said that if a woman prays with this part of her body uncovered, she dishonors it. (1 Cor. 11:5)

19 Paul taught that the woman is not without this other half in the Lord. (1 Cor. 11:11)

22 The woman who touched the hem of Christ's garment was healed of an issue of this life-giving substance. (Matt. 9:20)

23 According to the Gospel of St. John, how many women named Mary stood by the cross? (John 19:25)

25 The Syrophenician Greek woman that petitioned Jesus to heal her daughter was of the people of this country. (Matt. 15:22; Mark 7:26)

27 Jesus said that the woman who touched the hem of His garment was healed because she exhibited this power. (Matt. 9:22)

Down

2 When the Syrophenician woman petitioned Jesus to heal her daughter, the disciples pled with Him to send her where? (Matt. 15:23)

4 Jesus told the woman at the well that those who would drink of His living water would never experience this. (John 4:14)

6 Paul taught that women should only ask questions of these companions. (1 Cor. 14:35)

7 This was the name of the wife of Ananias. She died because she lied to the Holy Ghost. (Acts 5:1)

8 What was the name of the wife of Felix? (Acts 24:24)

9 When king Agrippa came to ques-

tion Paul, this was the name of the woman that was with him. (Acts 25:23)

11 Paul states that Eve was in transgression because she was this. (1 Tim. 2:14)

12 This is the total number of virgins in the parable of the virgins. (Matt. 25:1)

13 This Apostle's wife's mother was healed by Jesus. (Matt. 8:14–15)

16 Paul advised that widows under this age should not be taken into the church. (1 Tim. 5:9)

18 Peter's first denial of Jesus was precipitated by the question asked by a damsel who was the keeper of this opening. (John 18:17)

20 This was the object lost by the woman in the parable, for which she swept her house. (Luke 15:8)

21 When the Syrophenician woman petitioned Jesus to heal her daughter, it was because her daughter was vexed with what? (Matt. 15:22; Mark 7:26)

24 Paul taught that when this is very long, it is glory unto a woman, for it is a covering for her. (1 Cor. 11:15)

26 This prophetess testified to the baby Jesus' divinity in the temple. (Luke 2:36)

262. Jesus prohibited Mary Magdalene from what, when she first saw Him after the resurrection? (John 20:17)

263. What was the name of the adulterous woman Herod was living with as wife? (Matt. 14:3)

264. Paul said that man is the glory of God, the woman is the glory of whom? (1 Cor. 11:7)

265. Paul states that women should adorn themselves in what type of apparel? (1 Tim. 2:9)

266. After anointing Jesus' feet, what did Mary wipe them with? (John 12:3)

267. What is the name of the woman Peter raised from the dead? (Acts 9:40)

268. What did the woman pour on Jesus' head as He sat at meat? (Matt. 26:7)

269. After the Sabbath, who was the first to go to the sepulcher where they had placed the body of Jesus? (Matt. 28:1)

270. Martha secretly called what person to come to Jesus, after she met Him? (John 11:28)

271. Why was the woman taken in adultery brought to Jesus? (John 8:6)

272. Which chapter in 1 Corinthians talks about women?

273. Paul said husbands (to please their spouses) care for the things of the what? (1 Cor. 7:33)

274. According to Paul, we are not to be unequally yoked together with whom? (2 Cor. 6:14)

275. Paul directed that a man and wife were to leave who and become one flesh? (Eph. 5:31)

276. Jesus said Moses had allowed divorce because of the hardness of the Israelites' what? (Matt. 19:8)

277. Jesus was asked if a husband could "_____ _____ his wife for every cause." (Matt. 19:3)

278. Who does Paul say is sanctified by the believing wife? (1 Cor. 7:14)

279. Paul says it is better to marry than to do what? (1 Cor. 7:9)

280. The husband is the head of the wife, as Christ is the head of the what? (Eph. 5:23)

281. In a question Jesus was asked concerning the resurrection, the example was used of a woman who married several brothers as each in turn died. How many brothers did she marry altogether? (Matt. 22:25)

---

282. Peter says husbands should give honor to their wives, as unto what kind of vessel? (1 Pet. 3:7)

283. Husbands should love their wives as Christ loved the what? (Eph. 5:25)

284. What was the name of the husband of Sapphira? (Acts 5:1)

285. Paul taught that deacons should be the husbands of how many wives? (1 Tim. 3:12)

286. What did the ten virgins take with them as they went forth to meet the bridegroom? (Matt. 25:1)

287. What was the sign to Zacharias that his wife would have a child? (Luke 1:20)

288. Paul states that bishops should have how many wives? (1 Tim. 3:2)

True or False?

1260. Jesus warned His disciples to beware of the leaven of the Pharisees and the scribes. (Matt. 16:6)

289. Paul said that he had begotten (baptized) what person in his bonds? (Philem. 1:10)

290. What was the "eternal" request of the mother of Zebedee's children? (Matt. 20:20–21)

291. Paul taught that the children of a bishop should be in what, to him? (1 Tim. 3:4)

292. It would be better if what were hanged around your neck, than you offend a little child? (Matt. 18:6)

293. According to Paul, we are to walk as children of what? (Eph. 5:8)

294. How old were the children Herod slew when he tried to kill the baby Jesus? (Matt. 2:16)

295. Paul said we are what, to the adoption of children by Jesus? (Eph. 1:5)

296. In the Beatitudes, which "blessed" are called the children of God? (Matt. 5:9)

297. Paul taught that if you have what attribute, you are of the children of Abraham? (Gal. 3:7)

Solution on page 279

Across

1 Bernice accompanied this King to see the incarcerated Paul. (Acts 25:23)

6 Scholars often refer to the brother of Jude, who was an Apostle, as James the _____. (Mark 15:40)

8 In the circumstances of the healing of the man born blind, who did Jesus say had sinned, the man or his parents? (John 9:3)

9 Paul refers to Titus as this family relation. (Titus 1:4)

10 Jesus said that no man knows the Son, but this relation. (Matt. 11:27)

12 Paul taught that if a man cannot govern this symbolic word (a dwelling place that is used to describe his family), he cannot rule in the church. (1 Tim. 3:5)

13 This Apostle had a mother-in-law. (Matt. 8:14)

14 Paul taught that fathers should NOT provoke these to wrath. (Eph. 6:4)

19 This was the relationship between Mary and Elisabeth (plural). (Luke 1:36)

20 Who said to call no man father upon the earth? (Matt. 23:1, 9)

21 Peter's wife's mother was healed by Jesus of this malady. (Matt. 8:15)

23 The Jews took testimony from these relations concerning the healing of the one born blind. (John 9:20)

25 If a son asks for bread, a man would not give him this hard object. (Matt. 7:9)

26 Paul taught that children provoked to anger by their fathers will become this. (Col. 3:21)

Down

2 Paul stated that the fathers of our flesh corrected us, and we gave them this. (Heb. 12:9)

3 This is the name of the Apostle Peter's brother who was also an Apostle. (Matt. 4:18)

4 This relation of Paul's told him of the conspiracy to kill him. (Acts 23:16)

5 This was the brother of John. He was also an Apostle. (Matt. 4:21)

7 This woman was the mother of Timothy. (2 Tim. 1:5)

11 This was the relationship between Herod the tetrarch and Philip (plural). (Matt. 14:3)

15 This woman was the grandmother of Timothy. (2 Tim. 1:5)

16 Paul taught that those led by the Spirit of God are the sons of this Supreme Being. (Rom. 8:14)

17 This word was used to describe the undefiled daughters of Philip the evangelist who prophesied. (Acts 21:9)

18 This was the father of James and John. (Matt. 4:21)

20 This was the brother of James the son of Zebedee. (Matt. 4:21)

22 Was the Apostle Peter married? (Matt. 8:14)

24 How many children of Philip the evangelist prophesied? (Acts 21:9)

Trick Question

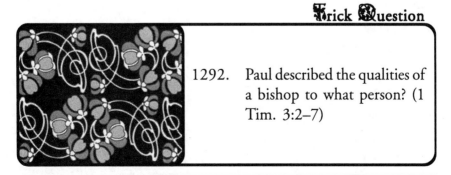

1292. Paul described the qualities of a bishop to what person? (1 Tim. 3:2–7)

298. During His trials, what words did Jesus speak before Herod? (Luke 23:9)

299. What was Herod's decree when he tried to kill the baby Jesus? (Matt. 2:16)

300. What was the reason the wise men did not return to Herod after their visit with the Christ child? (Matt. 2:12)

301. What was Herod's question to the wise men as they left him to find the baby Jesus? (Matt. 2:7)

302. What Apostle did Herod kill with a sword? (Acts 12:2)

303. How did the Herod of the book of Acts die? (Acts 12:23)

304. Although it made Herod sorrowful, he beheaded John the Baptist for the sake of his what? (Matt. 14:9)

305. Who did Herod think Jesus was? (Matt. 14:2)

306. What Jewish ruler came to Jesus by night to question Him? (John 3:1)

307. Many leaders believed on Jesus, but did not follow Him, for fear of what? (John 12:42)

308. What did the Jewish rulers do to the Apostles after Peter healed the lame man? (Acts 4:17)

309. Where did the Jewish Rulers love to have the "chief seats"? (Matt. 23:6)

310. Whose influence did Stephen say the council resisted, as did their fathers? (Acts 7:51)

311. What was the reaction of the Apostles to their beating by the council? (Acts 5:41)

312. Who was king of Israel at the time of the birth of Jesus? (Matt. 2:1)

313. Which member of the Sanhedrin brought myrrh and aloes to adorn Christ's dead body? (John 19:39)

314. After being healed, the man born blind was taken to which Jewish rulers? (John 9:13)

315. In the parable of the unmerciful servant, the unmerciful servant begged the king to have patience and he would pay him what amount? (Matt. 18:26)

316. Who reigned in Judea after the death of Herod the Great? (Matt. 2:22)

RULERS MATCH GAME
Who Are The Players?

Match the questions on the left with the answers on the right.
The solution is on page 294.

A. This Sanhedrin member defended Jesus to the council. (John 7:50–51)

Rooms

B. After the raising of Lazarus, some told these Jewish Rulers about it. (John 11:46)

Sepulchers

C. This man was the king of Damascus at the time of Paul. (2 Cor. 11:32)

Herod

D. The words of Stephen at his trial, cut the council to this internal organ. (Acts 7:54)

Candace

E. The Ethiopian eunuch baptized by Philip was the servant to this queen. (Acts 8:27)

Nicodemus

F. The Pharisees were compared to these whited burial places. (Matt. 23:27)

Roman

G. Because of Paul's teaching, the Greeks beat this chief ruler of the synagogue. (Acts 18:17)

Pharisees

H. Jesus reminded the Rulers that under their Law, the testimony of how many men is true. (John 8:17)

Aretas

I. Pilate sent Jesus to this Jewish ruler for interrogation. (Luke 23:4, 7)

Sosthenes

J. The chief captain became afraid for his own safety after Paul told him he was of this citizenship. (Acts 22:29)

Two

K. The Jewish Rulers loved to be seated in the uppermost of these locations at their feasts. (Matt. 23:6)

Heart

317. What was Pilate's sign to the crowd to rid himself of Christ's blood? (Matt. 27:24)

318. Jesus declared to Pilate that His kingdom was not of this what? (John 18:36)

319. What did Pilate give the Rulers of the Jews in order to secure the sepulcher where the body of Jesus lay? (Matt. 27:65)

320. What is the name of the hall where Jesus was mocked after His last trial before Pilate? (Mark 15:16–20)

321. What was the dialectic question Pilate asked Jesus? (John 18:38)

322. What did Pilate's wife have that involved Jesus during His trial before Pilate? (Matt. 27:19)

323. Who begged Pilate for the body of Jesus after His death? (Matt. 27:57–58)

324. What was Pilate's question to Jesus concerning kingship? (Matt. 27:11)

325. How did Pilate punish Jesus before the crucifixion? (John 19:1)

326. Paul said that he had been given a what, in the flesh? (2 Cor. 12:7)

327. If Jesus is the vine, who are the branches? (John 15:5)

328. Paul taught that the Gentiles and the Jews were compared to a wild and tame what? (Rom. 11:17–24)

329. Who climbed a tree to see Jesus pass? (Luke 19:2–4)

330. What was John the Baptist to lay at the root of the tree if it did not bring forth fruit? (Matt. 3:10)

331. If the Father is the husbandman, who is the vine? (John 15:1)

332. Paul taught that the Gentiles were considered what kind of a "wild" tree? (Rom. 11:17)

333. What kind of tree did the short man climb so that he could see the Savior as He passed? (Luke 19:2–4)

334. What is the meaning of the name Emmanuel? (Matt. 1:23)

335. What is the interpretation of the word "Cephas"? (John 1:42)

336. How did the blind men at Jericho address Jesus? (Matt. 20:30)

337. What was the new name given by the Lord to Simon Barjona? (Matt. 16:17–18)

338. What is the name of Andrew's brother who was one of the Twelve Apostles? (Matt. 4:18)

339. What name of Christ signifies both the beginning and the end? (Rev. 1:8)

340. What is another name for the Comforter? (John 14:26)

341. What is the common name of the parable that warns against covetousness? (Luke 12:16–21)

342. What was the name of the Apostle that first entered the Savior's sepulcher on the morning of the resurrection? (John 20:6)

343. Which parable is named after a wayward son? (Luke 15:11–32)

344. What person was called to be an Apostle at the same time as Saul? (Acts 13:2)

345. What does John state is another name for the Sea of Tiberias? (John 6:1)

346. What disease did Simon of Bethany have? (Matt. 26:6)

347. What is the name of the blind man that was healed at Jericho? (Mark 10:46)

348. The Feast of unleavened bread was also called what? (Matt. 26:2, 17)

True or False?

1261. According to Jude, Michael and the devil contended over the resurrection. (Jude 1:9)

MEN MATCH GAME #2

Who Are The Players?

*Match the questions on the left with the answers on the right.
The solution is on page 289.*

A. If we have opportunity, we should al-
    ways do this. (Gal. 6:10)   Four thousand

B. Paul taught that by man came death
    and by man also came this. (1 Cor.   Tame it
    15:21)

C. Pilate offered to free Jesus, but the
    Jews chose to free this man instead.   Bishop
    (John 18:40)

D. Paul said when we become men, we
    should put away these things. (1 Cor.   Unstable
    13:11)

E. Things of God are foolishness to this
    man. (1 Cor. 2:14)   Childish things

F. James taught that a man that is double
    this, is unstable in all his ways. (James   Good
    1:8)

G. There were this many men at the sec-
    ond feeding of the multitude. (Matt.   Minded
    15:38)

H. James taught that no man can do this
    to the tongue. (James 3:8)   Resurrection

I. A double minded man is this in all his
    ways. (James 1:8)   Barabbas

J. Paul taught that a man desires a good
    work if he desires this office. (1 Tim.
    3:1)   Natural man

Challenged by the New Testament   77

NAMES WORD SEARCH
Who Are The Players?

Solution on page 290

```
K  R  T  B  A  R  T  H  O  L  O  M  E  W  N  J
W  K  Y  J  Z  A  C  H  A  R  I  A  S  K  S  U
Q  N  G  N  E  R  N  E  P  L  M  N  B  A  Y  D
M  V  T  W  E  S  T  H  S  T  K  X  M  J  N  A
W  G  T  T  G  A  U  A  P  C  D  Y  H  O  T  S
Z  Q  E  P  L  A  B  S  T  N  L  B  Y  H  T  I
L  P  D  I  L  B  M  S  T  E  D  R  M  N  J  S
N  T  P  T  A  A  A  A  H  A  K  X  R  M  U  C
A  N  G  R  R  I  Z  D  L  C  B  F  L  A  S  A
T  L  A  N  N  T  P  A  F  I  L  I  L  R  T  R
H  B  P  A  T  T  H  Z  R  Y  E  E  T  K  U  I
A  Y  N  N  Y  L  D  W  C  U  L  L  O  H  S  O
N  A  J  N  T  T  B  H  H  Y  S  O  Q  P  A  T
A  K  K  M  N  F  F  M  J  N  H  I  B  N  A  K
E  L  B  A  R  N  A  B  U  S  T  S  A  U  L  S
L  T  H  E  O  P  H  I  L  U  S  T  K  T  Y  T
```

- This Apostle cut off the ear of Malchus during the arrest of Jesus. (John 18:10)

- This was Paul's previous name. (Acts 13:9)

- This is the name of one of the two travelers to whom the Lord appeared on the road to Emmaus after His resurrection. (Luke 24:18)

- This is the name of Timothy's grandmother. (2 Tim.1:5)

- This is another name of Barjesus the sorcerer. (Acts 13:6, 8)
  - (a) Elijah
  - (b) Thomas
  - (c) Elymas

- Jesus said this man was slain between the temple and the altar. (Matt. 23:35)

- This is the interpretation of the name Dorcas. (Acts 9:36)

  (a) Tabitha
  (b) Elisabeth
  (c) Judith

- When Barnabas and Saul returned to Jerusalem from their mission, they reported that they had taken this person with them. (Acts 12:25)

- This is the name of the disciple in Damascus who was told to heal Saul. (Acts 9:10)

- When Paul and Barnabus divided and went their own way, who took John Mark? (Acts 15:39)

- This is the name of the brother of Mary and Martha. (John 11:1–2)

- This was the surname of Barsabas. (Acts 1:23)

- Jesus described this person as an Israelite in whom there was no guile. (John 1:47)

- This was the Roman governor of Palestine at Jesus' time. (Matt. 27:2)

- This was the individual to whom the book of Acts was apparently written. (Acts 1:1)

- This is the Apostle that is always listed last. (Matt. 10:4)

- This is the name of the Jewish leader who spoke of caution in acting against the Apostles. (Acts 5:34)

- This is the name of the person released by Pilate in Christ's stead. (Matt. 27:21)

- It is the conclusion of most scholars that this is the other name of the Apostle Nathanael. (Matthew 10:3; Mark 3:18; John 1:45)

- When Jesus was arrested He asked, "Whom seek ye?" They answered "_____ of Nazareth." (John 18:5)

Trick Question

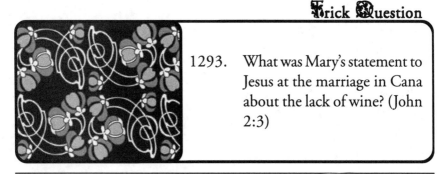

1293. What was Mary's statement to Jesus at the marriage in Cana about the lack of wine? (John 2:3)

349. According to Paul, as fellow citizens and Saints, we are of the what, of God? (Eph. 2:19)

350. Peter described the Saints as being what, made special by the foreknowledge of God? (1 Pet. 1:2)

351. Paul taught that the Saints would judge what? (1 Cor. 6:2)

352. Paul declared that he did NOT want the Roman Saints to be what? (Rom. 1:13)

353. What were the Saints at Antioch first called? (Acts 11:26)

354. John the Revelator declared that he was a companion in what, with the Saints? (Rev. 1:9)

355. Peter said we are a chosen generation and a royal what? (1 Pet. 2:9)

356. The Grecian members of the church murmured against the Hebrew members for neglecting whom? (Acts 6:1)

357. Paul said there were to be no what, between the Corinthian Saints? (1 Cor. 1:10)

358. Who accounted himself less than the least of all saints? (Eph. 3:8)

359. The Corinthian Saints were bragging about different men who had done what for them? (1 Cor. 1:12, 14)

360. According to Paul, we are no more strangers and foreigners, but what with the Saints? (Eph. 2:19)

361. Paul said that he had been informed of the contentions among the Corinthian Saints by those of the house of whom? (1 Cor. 1:11)

362. John told the Saints not to marvel if what entity hated them? (1 John 3:13)

363. John addresses the Saints as his little what? (1 John 2:1)

True or False?

1262. Paul said that a man should leave his father and mother and cleave unto his wife and thereafter live together as one couple. (Eph. 5:31)

Imagination Is
Everything

364. Is it true that Paul said God, in past times, winked at idolatry and ignorance? (Acts 17:16, 30)

365. Paul exhorted the Thessalonians to abstain from even the what, of evil? (1 Thes. 5:22)

366. What happened to the fig tree Jesus cursed? (Matt. 21:19)

367. What (besides milk), did Paul say belonged to those of full age? (Heb. 5:13–14)

368. Jesus declared that the harvest was plenteous, but the what were few? (Matt 9:37)

369. Jesus said that He only did that which He had seen what person do? (John 5:19)

370. As a teaching example, Jesus posed: if a son asks for a fish, what man would give him a what? (Matt. 7:10)

371. If Jesus is the vine, what are the Apostles? (John 15:5)

372. Jesus declared that the Pharisees were the blind leaders of whom? (Matt. 15:14)

373. What type of water did Jesus promise the Samaritan woman by the well? (John 4:10)

---

374. The Pharisees enlarged the borders of their what, to be seen of men? (Matt. 23:5)

375. Jesus would gather the chosen children of Jerusalem as a hen would gather what? (Matt. 23:37)

376. What chapter in Galatians lists the fruits of the Spirit?

377. Jesus said that God would clothe the Apostles as He clothed the _____ of the field. (Matt. 6:30)

378. What was the prophesied sign that concluded Peter's denials? (Matt. 26:34)

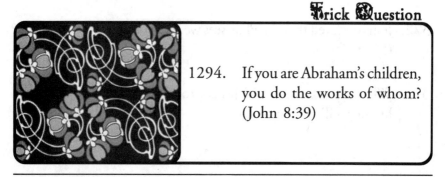

Trick Question

1294. If you are Abraham's children, you do the works of whom? (John 8:39)

379. What type of generation seeks after signs? (Matt. 12:39)

380. What was on the "sheet" Peter saw in his vision? (Acts 10:12, 14)

381. Who paid Melchizedek "a tenth part of all"? (Heb. 7:1–2)

382. What abomination did Daniel prophesy would happen before the end? (Matt. 24:15)

383. Who did Jesus declare was the greatest prophet that had been born of woman? (Matt. 11:11)

384. As a refutation to Jesus' claim that the truth would make them free, the Jews maintained that they were from the seed of which ancient prophet? (John 8:33)

385. What was the "sign" Agabus gave of Paul's prophesied fate at Jerusalem? (Acts 21:11)

386. What was the prophecy of Isaiah that was fulfilled by the healings of Jesus? (Matt. 8:17)

387. Paul said that the gospel had been preached to what Old Testament person, who was the father of the Hebrew race? (Gal. 3:8)

388. Prophecy came in olden times as holy men were moved upon by what, according to Peter? (2 Pet. 1:21)

389. Who did Jesus say was the Elias that was to come? (Matt. 11:13–14)

390. What did Paul prophesy concerning his pending voyage to Rome? (Acts 27:10)

391. Which ancient prophet did Jesus say had seen his day and was glad? (John 8:56)

IMAGERY WORD SEARCH
Imagination Is Everything

Solution on page 282

```
X  W  X  B  T  R  U  M  P  E  T  L  T
M  A  V  R  W  K  E  L  F  P  Z  N  Q
W  R  P  A  M  H  G  Y  E  A  A  L  R
G  M  M  N  N  B  I  N  E  T  L  L  H
C  O  X  C  D  K  O  T  A  Z  X  S  R
B  U  C  H  G  T  C  S  E  S  B  B  E
D  R  H  E  S  M  J  Q  R  H  Y  S  L
G  L  A  S  S  N  W  E  T  W  S  L  L
N  R  R  V  N  M  Y  A  S  A  P  I  P
P  Q  I  N  G  A  E  L  L  U  X  G  Q
F  M  T  T  R  D  G  G  N  H  S  H  G
M  B  Y  P  K  M  S  W  O  R  D  T  L
C  A  N  D  L  E  S  T  I  C  K  S  Z
```

- Paul declared that this reigned from Adam to Moses. (Rom 5:14)

- In John the Revelator's vision, John saw a sea of this mingled with fire. (Rev. 15:2)
  - (a) glass
  - (b) monsters
  - (c) boats

- He is the good shepherd in the good shepherd discourse. (John 10:7, 11)

- If Jesus is the vine, the Apostles are these. (John 15:5)
  - (a) trunks
  - (b) branches
  - (c) fruit

- We cannot think of the Godhead as like unto gold, silver, and this. (Acts 17:29)

- Men light candles to put them on these. (Matt. 5:15)
  - (a) holders
  - (b) windows
  - (c) candlesticks

- The light of the body is this. (Matt. 6:22)
  - (a) spirit
  - (b) eye
  - (c) Son

- Paul said that we should put on the whole what of God? (Eph. 6:11)

- Paul declares that the God of peace will bruise this under our feet. (Rom. 16:20)

  (a) power
  (b) death
  (c) Satan

- Christ did not come to send peace, but this to the earth. (Matt. 10:34)

  (a) war
  (b) problem
  (c) sword

- Jesus declared that He was the way, the means, and the life (true or false). (John 14:6)

- We are as sounding brass and a tinkling symbol if we have not this. (1 Cor. 13:1)

- Paul questions who will prepare for the battle if an uncertain sound comes from this instrument. (1 Cor. 14:8)

- Paul said we now see through this darkly. (1 Cor. 13:12)

  (a) mirror
  (b) window
  (c) glass

- After teaching the woman by the well, Jesus told his disciples that the fields were this color and ready for harvest. (John 4:35)

- Peter taught that we are called out of darkness into His marvelous what? (1 Pet. 2:9)

- Jesus said that the scribes made these long as a "pretense" of their righteousness. (Mark 12:40)

  (a) prayers
  (b) faces
  (c) sermons

True or False?

1263. According to Paul, he that loveth his wife hateth himself. (Eph. 5:28)

SIGNS AND VISIONS
Imagination Is Everything

Solution on page 297

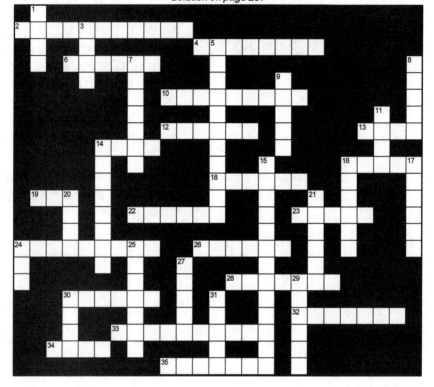

Across

2 Paul taught that the wisdom of the world is this with God. (1 Cor. 3:19)

4 Paul prophesied that all things in Christ were to be gathered together in one in the dispensation of this "completeness" of times. (Eph. 1:10)

6 Paul prophesied that after he departed, these grievous animals would enter the flock. (Acts 20:29)

10 Paul went to this country because of a vision. (Acts 16:9)

12 This is the number of times Peter saw the Cornelius "sheet vision" while he was on the rooftop. (Acts 10:16)

13 Paul declared that the Corinthians were to greet one another with this holy ritual. (1 Cor. 16:20)

14 Paul said God would send delusions, and the unrighteous would believe these untruths. (2 Thes. 2:11)

16 The Jews asked Jesus for a sign. He said there would be no sign given

but the sign of this prophet. (Matt. 12:39)

18 Jesus said that this Old Testament prophet had been fulfilled with the coming of John the Baptist. (Matt. 3:3)

19 Before the Cornelius "sheet vision," Peter went to this "apex" of the house to rest. (Acts 10:9)

22 Paul told Timothy that in latter times, some would depart from the faith by giving heed to doctrines of these. (1 Tim. 4:1)

23 The Jews trusted in this Old Testament Law giver, and Jesus said the man would eventually accuse them to the Father. (John 5:45)

24 Paul warned that in the latter-days, men would have a form of this, but deny the power thereof. (2 Tim. 3:5)

26 Paul taught that latter-day men would be lovers of their own what? (2 Tim. 3:2)

28 A prophet is not accepted as a prophet in his own _____ . (Luke 4:24)

30 Beware of false prophets clothed in this animals clothing. (Matt. 7:15)

32 The Jews asked Jesus if He was greater than this dead prophet and patriarch. (John 8:53)

33 Paul taught that godly sorrow works this. (2 Cor. 7:10)

34 The wise men were given a sign of Christ's birth by seeing this new light in the heavens. (Matt. 2:2)

35 Peter learned from his vision, and from Cornelius, that God was no respecter of these. (Acts 10:34)

Down

1 John the Revelator beheld in his vision that this was opened to him in heaven. (Rev. 4:1)

3 Paul states that latter-day apostates will have their conscience's seared with this hot household implement. (1 Tim. 4:2)

5 Paul said that the gift of tongues was a sign for these who questioned. (1 Cor. 14:22)

7 Paul taught that Abraham received "the promise" from God after he had patiently _____. (Heb. 6:15)

8 Jesus said that John the Baptist was one witness, but even a greater witness were these that He performed. (John 5:36)

9 Paul warned Timothy that in the last days these perilous calculations would come. (2 Tim. 3:1)

11 The Lord taught that a wicked and adulterous generation seeks after this. (Matt. 16:4)

14 Paul said latter-day men would be ever doing this educational thing, but never able to come to the knowledge of the truth. (2 Tim. 3:7)

15 Abraham believed God, and it was counted unto him for this. (Rom. 4:3)

16 This Old Testament prophet was fulfilled in Herod's slaying of the children. (Matt. 2:17, 18)

17 Paul said that although the Philippians would believe, they would also do this for Christ's sake. (Philip 1:29)

20 This person asked Jesus, "Who art thou, Lord?" when He appeared to

him in vision on the road to Damascus. (Acts 9:5)

21 Jesus declared that in His own country, a prophet was without this. (Matt. 13:57)

24 James taught that Abraham was called a friend of this Deity. (James 2:23)

25 The council did this to their ears when Stephen testified of his vision. (Acts 7:57)

27 At Christ's death, the temple veil was rent in this manner from top to bottom. (Matt. 27:51)

29 Before Peter received the Cornelius "sheet vision," he fell into this. (Acts 10:10)

30 Jesus said that the scribes and Pharisees sat correctly in this symbolic "chair" of Moses' leadership. (Matt. 23:2)

31 Paul taught that in the latter-days, some who did not believe would command to abstain from these. (1 Tim. 4:3)

Trick Question

1295. Paul said that if you sin without law, you shall perish without what? (Rom. 2:12)

392. Peter describes wicked men as "brute beasts" that speak evil of things they do not what? (2 Pet. 2:12)

393. About how many swine did the demonic named Legion enter, after he was cast out of a man? (Mark 5:13)

394. The Lord called the Pharisees a generation of what? (Matt. 23:33)

395. The tail of what colorful animal drew away one-third of the stars of heaven? (Rev. 12:3–4)

396. When Jesus sent the Apostles forth, He commanded them to be as wise as what? (Matt. 10:16)

397. Paul said that he had been delivered out of the mouth of what beast? (2 Tim. 4:17)

398. What did the swine do after the evil spirits named Legion possessed them? (Matt. 8:32)

399. Christ declared He was sent only to the lost sheep of what house? (Matt. 15:24)

400. What is the common name of the parable that involved sheep? (Matt. 18:12–13)

401. Jesus said there were other what, than those of the Jewish fold? (John 10:16)

402. Jesus told the Syrophenician woman that the children's bread was not to be cast to what animals? (Matt. 15:26)

403. Through the miracle of the coin in the mouth of the fish, Jesus provided what for the temple tax? (Matt. 17:24–27)

404. What two Jewish groups did John the Baptist call a generation of vipers? (Matt. 3:7)

405. In the parable of the lost sheep, how many of the sheep did the shepherd seek? (Matt. 18:12)

406. The Apostles were admonished to be as harmless as what? (Matt. 10:16)

407. What did the serpent cast after the woman in John the Revelator's vision? (Rev. 12:15)

408. He that enters into the flock by the door of the sheepfold is called what? (John 10:1–2)

409. Jesus told the Syrophenician woman that He was sent only to the lost sheep of the house of _____. (Matt. 15:24)

410. Peter compares the devil to what animal seeking to devour? (1 Pet. 5:8)

411. What did Jesus say was easier to do than for a rich man to get into heaven? (Matt. 19:24)

412. Christ's sheep hear His what? (John 10:27)

413. In John the Revelator's vision, the beast from the sea had the feet of what animal? (Rev. 13:2)

414. In John the Revelator's vision, the beast from the sea had a mouth like what animal? (Rev. 13:2)

415. In John the Revelator's vision, the second beast had horns like a what? (Rev. 13:11)

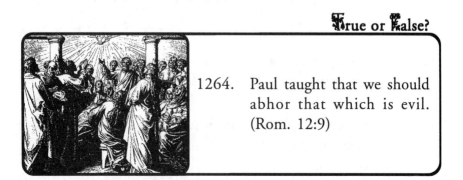

True or False?

1264. Paul taught that we should abhor that which is evil. (Rom. 12:9)

416. How many days did Jesus stay with the Samaritans after the incident with the woman at the well? (John 4:40)

417. What does Matthew say are "shortened" for the "elect's sake" before the Lord's coming? (Matt. 24:22)

418. Accused of drunkenness on the day of Pentecost, Peter said not so, because it is only what hour of the day? (Acts 2:15)

419. According to Peter, one day is as what to the Lord? (2 Pet. 3:8)

420. About what was the length of time between the deaths of Ananias and Sapphira? (Acts 5:7)

421. Paul first returned to Jerusalem how many years after his conversion? (Gal. 1:18)

422. How long had the impotent man by the pool of Bethesda been infirm? (John 5:5)

423. The healing of one born blind had not been heard of since when? (John 9:32)

424. How long had the woman who touched Christ's hem to be healed had an issue of blood? (Matt. 9:20)

425. Take no thought for tomorrow, for sufficient for today is the what thereof? (Matt. 6:34)

426. How long was Paul shipwrecked on Melita? (Acts 28:11)

427. The "great day" of the feast of tabernacles was which day? (John 7:37)

428. In John the Revelator's vision, how long was the beast given power? (Rev. 13:5)

429. According to Peter, one thousand years are as what to the Lord? (2 Pet. 3:8)

430. John states that no man could lay hands on Jesus because His what (an element of time), had not yet come? (John 7:30)

431. When the nobleman inquired, what was the hour his son had been healed? (John 4:52)

432. What day of the week was it when the disciples returned to the sepulcher (after the death of Jesus)? (John 20:1)

433. How long were the people with Jesus before the feeding of the five thousand occurred? (Mark 8:2)

434. On what day of the week did Jesus heal the one born blind? (John 9:14)

435. What did Jesus say He would do on the third day? (Matt. 20:19)

436. The angel told the Apostles as they watched Jesus ascend into heaven that the heavens must receive Jesus until the times of what? (Acts 3:21)

SYMBOLISM CROSSWORD
Imagination Is Everything

Solution on page 298

Across

2　We should not put this new material into old garments. (Matt. 9:16)

6　Jesus declared that He was the light of this orb. (John 8:12)

8　According to Paul, the word of God is sharper than this two-edged weapon. (Heb. 4:12)

11　Jesus said that those who did the will of this relation, were symbolically His mother, brothers, and sisters. (Matt. 12:50)

12　Peter declares Jesus was like a lamb without blemish and without this mark. (1 Pet. 1:19)

15　Paul said because of his infirmities he was made this, even when he was weak. (2 Cor. 12:10)

16　In the parable of the ten virgins, the foolish virgins were told when they knocked at the door: "I know you _____." (Matt. 25:12)

17　John the Revelator said that this new "identification" will be written upon the white stone that each will receive. (Rev. 2:17)

21　Paul said that all run the race, but only one receives this. (1 Cor. 9:24)

22　This, when new, should NOT be put into old bottles. (Matt. 9:17)

24　In the parable of the wheat and the tares, this good item represented the children of the kingdom. (Matt. 13:38)

25 Paul said that this Person was the first fruits of all that slept. (1 Cor. 15:20)

26 The name of the pale horse in John the Revelator's vision was death and this terrible place followed with him. (Rev. 6:8)

29 Satan is loosed after the one thousand years. These are the symbolic names of the nations from the four corners of the earth that he deceives. (Rev. 20:8)

Down

1 In John the Revelator's vision, the seven heads of the beast represented these seven high geological uprisings. (Rev. 17:9)

3 He that does evil hates this symbolic brightness. (John 3:20)

4 The leaven of the Pharisees was interpreted by the Lord as this. (Matt. 16:12)

5 In John the Revelator's vision, this is the name upon the crown on the head of the beast from the sea. (Rev. 13:1)

7 Jesus taught that if we symbolically eat and drink His flesh and blood, we will have this eternally. (John 6:54)

9 Jesus declared that He was the bread from heaven and if mankind would eat this bread, they would live forever. He said the Jewish fathers had eaten manna, but they were _____. (John 6:58)

10 You are not worthy of Christ unless you are willing to take up this. (Matt. 10:38)

13 John describes Jesus as the light that shines in this. (John 1:5)

14 Paul accounted his loss of all things as this waste. (Philip. 3:8)

18 When Jesus called Peter and Andrew from their nets, He said He would make them fishers of these. (Mark 1:17)

19 Agabus symbolically bound Paul with this personal item. (Acts 21:11)

20 Jesus declared that wherever this is, the eagles will be there also. (Matt. 24:28)

22 In John the Revelator's vision, this was the name of the star that came after the third angel "sounded." (Rev. 8:11)

23 Paul declared that the kingdom of God is not drink and this protein. (Rom. 14:17)

26 James states that this very small object is what ships are turned with. (James 3:4)

27 The potter has power over this material. (Rom. 9:21)

28 When told of Herod's threats against Him, Jesus compared Herod to this animal. (Luke 13:32)

437. James taught that this "little member," boasts great things. What is it? (James 3:5)

438. Which Apostle complained because Mary anointed Jesus' feet? (John 12:3–5)

439. Paul said that Jesus sat down on which hand of the Majesty on high? (Heb. 1:3)

440. Whose voice was heard from heaven as Jesus entered Jerusalem for the last Passover He would attended? (John 12:27–28)

441. What two personages contended over the body of Moses? (Jude 1:9)

442. What is the chapter in James regarding the tongue?

443. What did the woman with the issue of blood touch to be healed? (Matt. 9:20)

444. What did Jesus say was the light of the body? (Matt. 6:22)

445. Jesus healed two blind men when He did what to their eyes? (Matt. 9:28–30)

446. After the council heard Stephen speak, what did they do to him with their teeth? (Acts 7:54)

447. If your eye offends you, what are you to do? (Matt. 18:9)

448. What person did Paul say blinded the minds of nonbelievers? (2 Cor. 4:4)

449. Mary anointed the feet of Jesus with what? (John 12:3)

450. Paul taught that the eye cannot say what unto the hand? (1 Cor. 12:21)

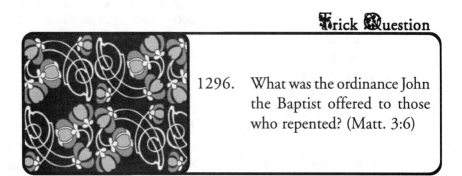

Trick Question

1296. What was the ordinance John the Baptist offered to those who repented? (Matt. 3:6)

Solution on page 275

Across

1 John ate the little book the angel gave him. In his mouth it was sweet, but when it entered his belly, his belly became this. (Rev. 10:10)

4 Righteousness is this part of the armor of God. (Eph. 6:14)

5 Foxes have holes, but Jesus declared that He had nowhere to lay this. (Matt. 8:20)

6 In the parable of Lazarus and the rich man, the rich man asked Lazarus to dip this digit into water and touch his tongue in order to cool it. (Luke 16:24)

7 Paul said we are saved by confessing with our _____, and believing with our heart. (Rom. 10:9)

11 Jesus said these parts of people's anatomy are dull of hearing. (Matt. 13:15)

12 In John the Revelator's vision of Jesus, Jesus had this many stars in His right hand. (Rev. 1:16)

13 For where your treasure is, there will this organ be also. (Matt. 6:21)

18 To quicken the death of the two thieves on the cross, the Romans broke these. (John 19:32)

19 Jesus said the good Shepherd gave this for His sheep. (John 10:11)

21 Paul declared that this part of the unrighteous man or woman is an open sepulcher. (Rom. 3:13)

24 The armor of God, girds these with truth. (Eph 6:14)

25 This part of everyone's anatomy will eventually confess that Jesus is Lord. (Philip. 2:11)

26 "It is a fearful thing to fall into the _____ of the living God." (Heb. 10:31)

29 Peter symbolically exhorted church members to gird up the loins of this thinking part of their bodies. (1 Pet. 1:13)

30 How beautiful are these lowest extremities of the body that belong to those who preach the gospel of peace. (Rom. 10:15)

31 Peter declared that we are redeemed by the part of Christ's body that flows through His veins. (1 Pet. 1:18–20)

32 We are both justified and condemned by these utterances. (Matt. 12:37)

Down

1 Jesus told the Apostles that His resurrected body was made of flesh and what else? (Luke 24:39)

2 The mote we see in others is lodged in this. (Matt. 7:3)

3 It is not the things that go into the mouth, but the things that come out of the mouth that defile this creation of God. (Matt. 15:11)

5 In John the Revelator's vision of Jesus, this is white as wool and snow. (Rev. 1:14)

6 When Stephen was condemned before the council, what about him appeared like that of an angel? (Acts 6:15)

8 John the Revelator declared that God would eventually wipe these away. (Rev. 7:17)

9 Salvation is this part of the armor of God that covers the head. (Eph. 6:17)

10 The gnashing of these bits of enamel, usually describes what occurs in outer darkness. (Matt. 8:12)

12 Peter taught that God is very pleased if this eternal part of our souls is meek and quiet. (1 Pet. 3:4)

14 The Jewish Rulers tried to entangle Jesus with this verbalization. (Matt. 22:15)

15 These fell from Saul's eyes when he was blessed by Ananias. (Acts 9:18)

16 Christ said we must symbolically eat this. He described it as bread. (John 6:51)

17 Jesus said the hour is coming when all the dead shall hear His what? (John 5:25)

20 Paul compares the different gifts of the Spirit with the members of this physical part of our soul. (1 Cor. 12:12)

22 Jesus could perceive these in men, even though they did not speak them. (Matt. 12:25)

23 Eventually, every man shall bow this at the name of Jesus. (Philip. 2:10)

27 Peter states that the end of our faith is the salvation of this (singlular). (1 Pet. 1:9)

28 Paul exhorted the young men to always be sober _____. (Titus 2:6)

451. Where did Jesus first see Matthew? (Matt. 9:9)

452. How many Epistles did Jude write?

453. What chapter in Matthew contains the Lord's prayer?

454. In what chapter of Luke is the intended genealogy of Jesus recorded?

455. Agrippa said that Paul almost persuaded him to be a what? (Acts 26:28)

456. Paul said that all must appear before what "seat"? (2 Cor. 5:10)

457. We should sing and make a melody in our what, to the Lord? (Eph. 5:19)

458. Paul said that we should salute one another with what? (Rom. 16:16)

459. The nine disciples (Apostles) could not do what to the lunatic child? (Matt. 17:14–18)

460. Who said: "For to me to live is Christ, and to die is gain?" (Philip. 1:21)

461. Were the Thessalonians righteous or unrighteous? (1 Thes. 1:8)

462. Who owned the tomb where Jesus' body was laid to rest? (Matt. 27:57, 60)

463. Communication more than yea and nay cometh of what? (Matt. 5:37)

464. What did the man do first with the hidden treasure, after he had found it? (Matt. 13:44)

465. If we help those who are hungry, thirsty, and naked, who do we help? (Matt. 25:35–40)

466. When Paul wrote to the Ephesians, he was a what, in Rome? (Eph. 3:1)

True or False?

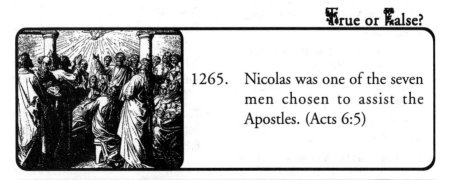

1265. Nicolas was one of the seven men chosen to assist the Apostles. (Acts 6:5)

EASY TRIVIA WORD SEARCH
Imagination Is Everything

Solution on page 278

```
T  D  L  R  R  I  G  H  T  E  O  U  S
D  C  G  K  C  A  I  A  P  H  A  S  M
T  X  B  Q  M  B  O  E  Z  T  J  V  H
D  H  M  P  X  N  L  O  X  J  B  K  R
A  G  E  L  K  T  T  N  H  S  D  Q  J
R  U  M  O  S  S  E  R  P  C  K  L
T  I  C  I  P  D  T  A  D  P  A  U  L
S  L  P  H  R  H  S  R  Q  N  H  J  K
E  E  W  O  A  E  I  F  I  M  Q  P  F
C  V  W  V  A  R  K  L  H  K  W  Z  A
P  P  I  C  M  Q  G  R  U  K  E  J  I
Y  N  Q  L  G  B  N  E  T  S  W  R  T
Y  J  U  P  I  T  E  R  R  F  J  N  H
```

- Had the Colossians ever seen Paul in person when he wrote his epistle to them? (Col. 2:1)

- Saul was also called by this new name. (Acts 13:9)

- To whom was the book of Acts addressed? (Acts 1:1)

- Paul wrote this number of Epistles to the Philippians.

- Whose superscription was on the tribute coin in the question posed to Jesus? (Matt. 22:20–21)

- This is what the people at Lystra named Barnabus. (Acts 14:12)

- Paul exhorted the Thessalonians that none render evil for this. (1 Thes. 5:15)

- Were the Colossians righteous or unrighteous? (Col. 1:4)

- Jesus declared that Nathanael was an Israelite in whom there was none of this. (John 1:47)

- Paul taught that bishops should not be given to wine, nor this, and not greedy of filthy lucre. (1 Tim. 3:3)

- Paul wrote one of these from Laodicea that the Colossians should read. (Col. 4:16)

- Annas was father-in-law to this high priest. (John 18:13)

- Paul declared that the just should live by this. (Rom. 1:17)

- Paul did not use flattering what, when writing to the Thessalonians. (1 Thes. 2:5)

- John the Baptist's head was brought to Herodias by her daughter in this. (Mark 6:28)

- The shield of faith can quench all these fiery instruments of the wicked. (Eph. 6:16)

Rules And Results

490. Paul said that as he prayed in the temple, he was in a what? (Acts 22:17)

491. James said that if any man lacks what quality, let him ask of God who gives liberally? (James 1:5)

492. Paul admonished the Thessalonians to pray without what? (1 Thes. 5:17)

493. What parable involving a friend was given to teach us to be persistent in prayer? (Luke 11:1, 5–8)

494. James says that God gives wisdom to all men and does not do what? (James 1:5)

495. James says we are to ask God in faith, nothing what? (James 1:6)

496. This parable involving prayer concerned a Pharisee and one from what other class of people? (Luke 18:10)

497. We are to ask in prayer believing, and if we do so, we are promised that we will receive what? (Matt. 21:22)

498. In the parable of the publican and the Pharisee at prayer in the temple, which man left the temple unjustified in the eyes of the Lord? (Luke 18:10–14)

467. What ordinance did Paul say he had performed for Crispus, Gaius, and the house of Stephanas at Corinth? (1 Cor. 1:14, 16)

468. According to Paul, the just are to live by what? (Gal. 3:11)

469. Paul taught, as tribulation worketh patience, so patience worketh what? (Rom. 5:4)

470. If we do not help the hungered, thirsty, and naked, who do we not help? (Matt. 25:41–46)

471. According to Paul, all things were created by whom? (Eph. 3:9)

472. Paul exhorted the Thessalonians to comfort whom? (1 Thes. 5:14)

473. Paul taught that where the testament is, there must be the what, of the testator? (Heb. 9:16)

474. According to Paul, we are justified by what? (Rom. 5:1)

475. Paul declared that we receive the atonement through what person? (Rom. 5:11)

476. Paul said there was one Lord, one what, and one baptism? (Eph. 4:5)

477. Jesus came not to call who to repentance, but the wicked? (Mark 2:17)

478. Paul taught that no man should put what kind of block in his brother's way? (Rom. 14:13)

479. Who does Paul state is the mediator between God and man? (1 Tim. 2:5)

480. Paul declared to the Romans that they who are of Israel by birth may not be children of the what? (Rom. 9:6–8)

481. Who are the two masters you cannot serve? (Matt. 6:24)

482. The doctrine of adoption is found in what chapter in Galatians?

483. Paul admonished Titus to speak what kind of doctrine when he was teaching? (Titus 2:1)

𝕋rick 𝕼uestion

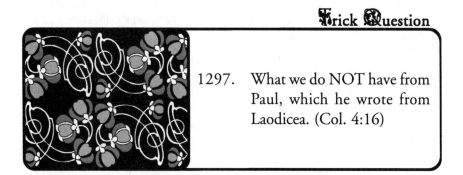

1297. What we do NOT have from Paul, which he wrote from Laodicea. (Col. 4:16)

DOCTRINE CROSSWORD
Rules And Results

Solution on page 277

Across

1 Heaven and earth will pass away, but this verbiage of Jesus will not pass away. (Matt. 24:35)

7 According to Paul, this shall keep your hearts and minds calm and passes all understanding. (Philip. 4:7)

8 Teaching the need for repentance, Paul symbolically instructs us to "put off" the old man, which is not pure, but this. (Eph. 4:22)

13 Jesus declared that if you keep His sayings, you will never see this final end. (John 8:51)

15 James said that we should not do this: neither by heaven, nor by earth, nor by oath. (James 5:12)

16 James said if we convert the sinner from the error of his ways, we will hide a multitude of these. (James 5:20)

17 Paul taught that you should entertain strangers, because you might be entertaining these beings unawares. (Heb. 13:2)

18 Paul said we should not be tossed to and fro by every what of doctrine? (Eph. 4:14)

19 Paul taught that the time would come when people would not endure sound doctrine, but would heap to

themselves teachers with ears that are this. (2 Tim. 4:3)

22 Paul taught that without those that lived before us, the Jews could not be made this. (Heb. 11:40)

23 Peter said we should add to our patience this celestial attribute? (2 Pet. 1:6)

Down

1 We who are strong should bear the infirmities of these who are not strong. (Rom. 15:1)

2 Jesus said that if the blind lead the blind, they will both fall into this deep depression. (Luke 6:39)

3 According to Paul, what communion hath light with this opposite. (2 Cor. 6:14)

4 Paul said there is one Lord, one faith, and one this. (Eph. 4:5)

5 Paul taught that Enoch was translated because of this? (Heb. 11:5)

6 Jesus began his ministry preaching repentance, saying that this kingdom and abode of God was at hand. (Matt. 4:17)

9 Jesus said that no one is "good," but whom? (Matt. 19:17)

10 Jesus said that if we know the truth, it will make us _____. (John 8:32)

11 Peter said that we should make sure our election and this. (2 Pet. 1:10)

12 Paul exhorted the Thessalonians to do this without ceasing. (1 Thes. 5:17)

14 James taught that pure religion is to visit the fatherless and these. (James 1:27)

20 Not only the truth, but this Person shall make you free. (John 8:36)

21 According to Paul, He is the mediator of the New Testament. (Heb. 9:14–15)

True or False?

1266. According to Paul, women should only ask their husbands questions at the Synagogue. (1 Cor. 14:35)

Solution on page 279

Q	D	M	O	N	T	H	N	L	I	F	E
X	I	V	D	P	S	R	X	C	E	V	L
F	S	G	P	N	A	C	R	C	X	I	W
B	P	K	I	R	B	T	N	Q	B	R	D
W	U	S	F	T	A	E	I	Y	D	T	J
N	T	G	L	D	D	Y	S	E	G	U	R
V	A	R	O	I	Y	T	E	S	N	E	K
M	T	G	V	B	I	R	K	R	P	C	Z
A	I	E	T	R	O	R	G	R	A	C	E
R	O	W	I	F	O	O	L	C	R	G	Q
R	N	P	M	W	Q	C	K	L	Z	M	R
Y	S	F	A	I	T	H	V	S	K	Z	M

- If we do not believe in Jesus, we will die in these. (John 8:24)
  - (a) sins
  - (b) sorrows
  - (c) needs

- James taught that this was dead and alone without works. (James 2:17)
  - (a) charity
  - (b) grace
  - (c) faith

- James taught that the trying of our faith works this. (James 1:3)
  - (a) happiness
  - (b) blessings
  - (c) patience

- Paul declared that in the latter-days, some who had departed from the faith would forbid some to do this. (1 Tim. 4:3)
  - (a) work
  - (b) eat meat
  - (c) marry

- James taught that faith without this is dead, being alone. (James 2:17)
  - (a) hope
  - (b) deeds
  - (c) works

- Paul declared that we are saved through faith by this. (Eph. 2:8)
  - (a) grace
  - (b) mercy
  - (c) justice

- Paul taught that we are to receive the weak in the faith, but not with these doubtful challenges. (Rom. 14:1)
  - (a) concerns
  - (b) disputations
  - (c) questions

- James said that the sick are saved through faith exercised by this. (James 5:15)
  - (a) prayer
  - (b) belief
  - (c) thanksgiving

- Paul taught that if you believe, you are no more a servant, but a son and an heir of this being through Christ. (Gal. 4:7)
  - (a) Jesus
  - (b) the Holy Ghost
  - (c) God

- Paul said faith is the substance of things hoped for and this proof of things not seen. (Heb. 11:1)
  - (a) testing
  - (b) facts
  - (c) evidence

- Paul taught that we are most miserable if we only have hope in Christ while we live in this period of time. (1 Cor. 15:19)
  - (a) world
  - (b) life
  - (c) existence

- Paul taught that some apostates shall depart from the faith, giving heed to these seducing influences. (1 Tim. 4:1)
  - (a) ghosts
  - (b) friends
  - (c) spirits

- The converts at Ephesus burned these tomes full of "curious arts" before men as evidence of their belief in Jesus. (Acts 19:19)
  - (a) statues
  - (b) scrolls
  - (c) books

- Peter said we should add this to our faith. (2 Pet. 1:5)
  - (a) virtue
  - (b) knowledge
  - (c) charity

- Paul taught that we will be saved if we believe with our heart and confess Jesus with this. (Rom. 10:9)
  - (a) heart
  - (b) mouth
  - (c) spirit

Trick Question

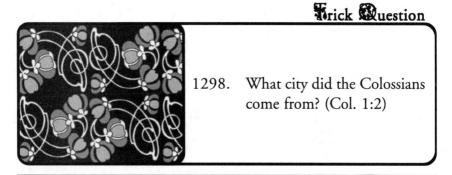

1298. What city did the Colossians come from? (Col. 1:2)

499. In what chapter in Galatians is the doctrine of justification of faith found?

500. What chapter in Hebrews is on the doctrine of faith?

501. What did the Lord declare was possible to him that believeth? (Mark 9:23)

502. What can you cast into the sea by faith? (Matt. 21:21)

503. Who was the person that caused Jesus to comment that He had not found such great faith in all Israel? (Matt. 8:5, 10)

504. According to James, a man is justified by his what, and not faith only? (James 2:24)

505. Doing works without faith causes one to stumble at what? (Rom. 9:32)

506. Paul said that after we believe, we are sealed with what? (Eph. 1:13)

507. To what small seed was faith compared? (Matt. 17:20)

508. Faith is which part of the armor of God? (Eph. 6:16)

509. Paul declared that you were justified by belief, and could not be justified by living what Law? (Acts 13:39)

484. Peter asked Jesus if it was correct that he forgive trespasses against him, how many times? (Matt. 18:21)

485. What did Jesus do when the scribes and Pharisees presented a woman taken in adultery to Him? (John 8:6)

486. What did the scribes accuse Jesus of because He forgave sins? (Matt. 9:3)

487. Who should be the first person to resolve a trespass? (Matt. 18:15)

488. When the adulteress was brought before Jesus, He told her accusers that he that was without sin should cast the first what? (John 8:7)

489. How often did Jesus say we should forgive one another? (Matt. 18:22)

True or False?

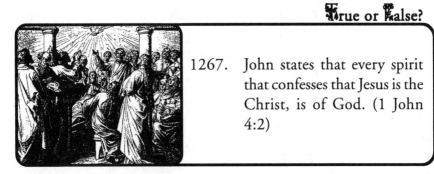

1267. John states that every spirit that confesses that Jesus is the Christ, is of God. (1 John 4:2)

ARMOR OF GOD
Rules And Results

Fill in the symbolic meaning for the armor shown below.
Use the questions on page 119 to help you.

527

526

525

523

522

524

521. We are to put on the armor of God so that we may stand the evil day and the _____ of the _____. (Eph. 6:11, 13)

522. In the armor of God, the loins are girded with what? (Eph. 6:14)

523. In the armor of God, the breastplate is what? (Eph. 6:14)

524. In the armor of God, the feet are shod with the preparation of the what? (Eph. 6:15)

525. In the armor of God, the shield represents what? (Eph. 6:16)

526. In the armor of God, the helmet is what? (Eph. 6:17)

527. In the armor of God, the sword represents the what? (Eph. 6:17)

528. Once we have on the whole armor of God, we are to pray always and watching with all _____ and _____ for all saints. (Eph. 6:18)

510. According to Paul, to whom did Abraham pay tithing? (Heb. 7:1–2)

511. God's commandment to honor one's parents was made of no effect by the Jews, because of their what? (Matt. 15:6)

512. If we keep the commandments, we shall abide in Jesus' what? (John 15:10)

513. "Thou shalt not kill" was changed to what? (Matt. 5:21–22)

514. After the resurrection, the Apostles were commanded to teach all nations and do what, in the name of the Father, the Son, and the Holy Ghost? (Matt. 28:19)

515. How many commandments are there upon which hangs all the law and the prophets? (Matt. 22:40)

516. What word was used by the Jews to free them from the fifth commandment? (Mark 7:11)

517. What is the second great commandment? (Matt. 22:39)

518. According to Paul, which is the first commandment with promise? (Eph. 6:2)

519. What is the first and great commandment in the law? (Matt. 22:36–37)

520. What did Jesus command the dead Lazarus to do? (John 11:43)

529. What did the Jews call Jesus for healing the one born blind on the Sabbath? (John 9:24)

530. The temple priests profane the Sabbath and are judged what? (Matt. 12:5)

531. Jesus declared that the Son of Man is what, even of the Sabbath day? (Matt. 12:8)

532. What did the women prepare, before returning to the tomb after the Sabbath, for the burial of the body of Christ? (Luke 23:56)

533. What requirement of the Law could the Jews perform on the Sabbath, even though performing it broke the law? (John 7:22–23)

534. What was the reaction of the Jewish leadership to Jesus healing on the Sabbath? (Matt. 12:14)

535. Why were the disciples of Jesus accused of Sabbath breaking as they walked with Him through a corn field? (Matt. 12:1–2)

Trick Question

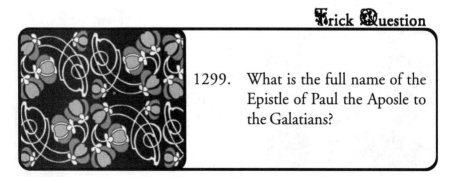

1299. What is the full name of the Epistle of Paul the Aposle to the Galatians?

536. When was the sacrament introduced by Jesus? (Matt. 26:26–27)

537. Who are we admonished to examine before taking the sacrament? (1 Cor. 11:28)

538. Paul said that because they were taking the sacrament unworthily, many at Corinth were what (choose one of three possible answers)? (1 Cor. 11:30)

539. The sacrament wine represents the what, of Christ? (Matt. 26:27–28)

540. What did the sacrament bread represent? (Matt. 26:26)

541. Eating and drinking the sacrament unworthily makes one guilty of what? (1 Cor. 11:27)

542. When Paul saw how the Corinthian Saints participated in the Lord's Supper he said, "_____ ye the church of God, and _____ them that have not?" (1 Cor. 11:20–22)

True or False?

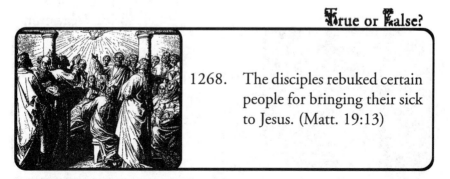

1268. The disciples rebuked certain people for bringing their sick to Jesus. (Matt. 19:13)

543. How many souls were baptized on Pentecost after Peter's sermon? (Acts 2:41)

544. Who baptized Jesus? (Matt. 3:13–16)

545. Why did Jesus go into the wilderness after His baptism? (Matt. 4:1)

546. Who asked Philip to baptize him as they rode in the carriage together? (Acts 8:27, 36)

547. Paul asked if the Ephesian disciples who had been baptized had been given what? (Acts 19:2)

548. What was John the Baptist's initial reaction when Jesus asked John to baptize Him? (Matt. 3:14)

549. As an argument for the resurrection, Paul asked why these beings were being baptized by proxy, if they rise not at all. Who are "these beings"? (1 Cor. 15:29)

550. What did the voice from heaven say immediately after Christ's baptism? (Matt. 3:17)

551. What descended upon Christ after His baptism? (Matt. 3:16)

552. What reason did Jesus gave for His baptism? (Matt. 3:15)

THE LAW CROSSWORD
Rules And Results

Solution on page 287

Across

3   Paul said that if you are justified by the law, you have fallen from this. (Gal. 5:4)

4   The wife is bound by the law so long as this person lives. (1 Cor. 7:39)

8   Paul said man is justified by this even without the deeds of the law. (Rom. 3:28)

9   Paul teaches that the law is good if men use it this way. (1 Tim. 1:8)

13   There was dissension between Paul and certain Judean men over this Mosaic requirement. (Acts 15:1–2)

14   Paul said man was NOT justified by these of the law, but by faith. (Gal 2:16)

15   Paul said that the scripture concluded that all were under this. (Gal. 3:22)

16   Jesus walked on this, and it defied the law of gravity. (Matt. 14:25)

20   The Law and these were in effect until John the Baptist. (Luke 16:16)

21   The Lord accused the Pharisees of omitting what type of "heavy" matters of the Law? (Matt. 23:23)

23   Paul said that where there is no law, this is not present. (Rom. 4:15)

Down

1   Paul said, "For the law made nothing _____." (Heb. 7:19)

2 Paul stated that he found a law: that when he would do good, this influence was always with him. (Rom. 7:21)

5 Paul declared that the Law was this kind of master to Israel. (Gal. 3:24)

6 James taught that if we keep the whole law (yet break one point) we are guilty of this amount. (James 2:10)

7 Paul taught that because the carnal mind is not subject to the law of God, it is this against God. (Rom. 8:7)

10 Paul said that through our faith we establish this. (Rom. 3:31)

11 Paul said if you boast of the law and break it, you do this to God (modern spelling). (Rom. 2:23)

12 Paul said that the doers of the law are this before God. (Rom. 2:13)

17 The Law will not pass away until every jot and this is fulfilled. (Matt. 5:18)

18 Paul said that hearers of the law were not justified before God, but these were. (Rom. 2:13)

19 John says that the Law was given by Moses, but grace and truth came by this person. (John 1:17)

22 Paul declared that the law is not made for which of God's righteous creations? (1 Tim. 1:9)

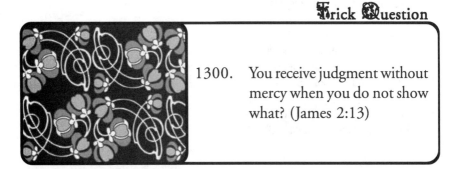

Trick Question

1300. You receive judgment without mercy when you do not show what? (James 2:13)

Match the questions on the left with the answers on the right.
The solution is on page 274.

A. This was the name of the first Gentile baptized by Peter. (Acts 10:31, 48)

Buried

B. The ancients were baptized unto Moses in the sea and in this. (1 Cor. 10:2)

Death

C. This was heard from heaven after the baptism of Jesus. (Matt. 3:17)

Cornelius

D. Being baptized unto Christ is as if you had been baptized unto His what? (Rom. 6:3)

Man

E. According to the King James Bible, did Jesus baptize people? (John 4:2)

Cloud

F. "Even baptism doth also now save us," like this number of people that were saved in the Ark. (1 Pet. 3:20–21)

Simon

G. Jesus came up out of the waters of baptism in this manner. (Matt. 3:16)

A voice

H. This sorcerer was baptized by Philip. (Acts 8:9, 13)

Eight

I. Through baptism we symbolically crucify this old person so that sin will be destroyed. (Rom. 6:6)

No

J. When we are baptized, we have been symbolically this with Christ. (Rom. 6:4)

Straightway

553. The Philippians were admonished to work out salvation with what? (Philip. 2:12)

554. Jesus declared to the Samaritan woman by the well that salvation was of what people? (John 4:22)

555. Paul said that we are not saved by works, lest any man should do what? (Eph. 2:9)

556. Peter said we should make our calling and what, sure? (2 Pet. 1:10)

557. Paul said that we are saved by grace, and it is a _____ of God. (Eph. 2:8)

558. Peter says that we are not redeemed with corruptible metals such as what? (1 Pet. 1:18)

559. Eternal life's gate is described as being what, and the way to eternal life is described as what? (Matt. 7:14)

560. According to Paul, corruption cannot inherit what? (1 Cor. 15:50)

561. Peter says that the salvation of your soul comes at the end of your what? (1 Pet. 1:9)

562. If who are scarcely saved, think what will happen to sinners? (1 Pet. 4:18)

563. Paul said Jesus, being made perfect, became the author of what? (Heb. 5:9)

564. Whosoever will save his life shall do what, with it? (Matt. 16:25)

565. Paul declares that if salvation is by works, then it is no more by what? (Rom. 11:6)

DEFINITIONS CROSSWORD
Rules And Results

Solution on page 277

Across

1 Paul declared that this virtue results from tribulation. (Rom. 5:3)

4 No man speaking by the Spirit of God calls Jesus _____. (1 Cor. 12:3)

7 Paul taught that the flesh and this other part of the soul are contrary to one another. (Gal. 5:17)

8 Paul declares there are diversities of these spiritual presents, but they are all of the same spirit. (1 Cor. 12:4)

10 Paul said that by cunning craftiness, men lie in wait to do this. (Eph. 4:14)

11 This is the interpretation of the word "Rabbi." (John 1:38)

12 Paul taught that we can do nothing against this, but only things for it. (2 Cor. 13:8)

14 The Lord said that a house divided against itself cannot do this. (Matt. 12:25)

16 Paul said there is nothing _____ in and of itself. (Rom. 14:14)

18 Paul said that to be spiritually minded is both this and peace. (Rom. 8:6)

19 Jesus said that whosoever commits this, is its servant. (John 8:34)

20 Paul declared that we should not be _____ in well doing. (2 Thes. 3:13)

Down

2 This is the meaning of the word "Corban." (Mark 7:11)

3 The Lord said that wisdom (speaking of it symbolically as a "mother") is justified of what offspring? (Matt. 11:19)

5 Paul taught that righteousness has no fellowship with this opposite. (2 Cor. 6:14)

6 This was the only legitimate reason for divorce that Jesus specifically identified. (Matt. 19:9)

8 Paul said he planted, Apollos watered, but this entity gave the increase. (1 Cor. 3:6)

9 This is the name of Jesus that means, "God with us." (Matt. 1:23)

13 Paul taught that if any would not work, neither should he do this. (2 Thes. 3:10)

15 Paul declared to the Hebrews that because they would not listen, their hearing became this. (Heb. 5:11)

17 Paul said that where there is no transgression, God has not given this. (Rom. 4:15)

True or False?

1269. Paul said that to have godliness with contentment is great gain. (1 Tim. 6:6)

566. What was the word Jesus spoke when He raised the daughter of Jairus from death? (Mark 5:41)

567. The Thessalonians were warned against "concupiscence," which means what? (1 Thes. 4:5; Dictionary definition.)

568. What is the meaning of the word "Ephphatha"? (Mark 7:34)

569. James says to count it joy, when we fall into divers what? (James 1:2)

570. What did Paul say God has provided for us, when we are tempted beyond our ability? (1 Cor. 10:13)

571. What kind of poison does Paul say is under the lips of the unrighteous? (Rom. 3:13)

572. Paul declares that evil communications corrupt what kind of manners? (1 Cor. 15:33)

573. According to Paul, the sting of death is what? (1 Cor. 15:56)

574. What person flees from the sheep when he sees the wolf coming? (John 10:12)

575. Jesus is the "propitiation" of our sins, what does this mean? (1 John 2:2; Dictionary defination)

576. Of what three things, does Paul say charity is the greatest? (1 Cor. 13:13)

577. Paul said that "he that soweth to the Spirit" shall reap everlasting what? (Gal. 6:8)

578. Paul said no man can say that Jesus is Lord, but by what? (1 Cor. 12:3)

579. Identify those He was referring to when Jesus said, "of such is the kingdom of heaven." (Matt. 19:14)

580. What is the meaning of, "Eli, Eli, lama sabachthani?" (Matt. 27:46)

Trick Question

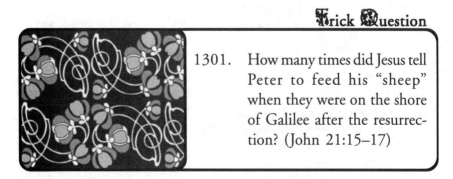

1301. How many times did Jesus tell Peter to feed his "sheep" when they were on the shore of Galilee after the resurrection? (John 21:15–17)

INSTRUCTIONS AND GOALS
Rules And Results

Solution on page 282

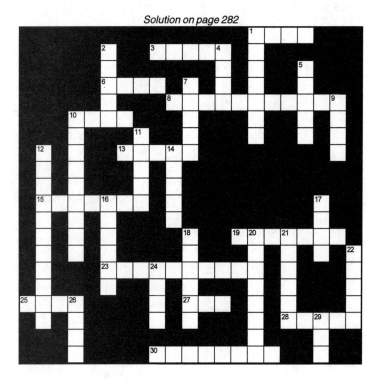

Across

1   Jesus said we would always have this class of people with us. (Matt. 26:11)

3   Paul instructed the Corinthians to covet earnestly these best presents. (1 Cor. 12:31)

6   Paul said that the sacrificial blood of bulls and goats cannot take away these. (Heb. 10:4)

8   Paul exhorted the Thessalonians to despise not this method of foretelling the future. (1 Thes. 5:20)

10 Before building a tower, you should count this. (Luke 14:28)

13 Paul told the Hebrews that the just should live by this attribute. (Heb. 10:38)

15 Paul declares that foolish and unlearned questions gender this. (2 Tim. 2:23)

19 James taught that when dealing fairly with people, we should not be respecters of these. (James 2:1–2)

23 Peter said we should add this modifier to our knowledge. (2 Pet. 1:6)

25 Paul taught that as tribulation works patience, and patience produces experience, so experience this (a synonym for belief). (Rom. 5:3–4)

27 The Lord said that our communication was to be only yea, and this. (Matt. 5:37)

28 The servant of the Lord, Paul said, must be patient and be able to do this. (2 Tim. 2:24)

30 Once Peter became "converted," Jesus said he should strengthen these male associates. (Luke 22:32)

Down

1 While they waited for Christ's coming, Paul admonished the Thessalonians to be this. (2 Thes. 3:5)

2 Paul declared that this Person had created all visible and invisible things. (Col. 1:16)

4 Paul warned that we must give earnest heed to things we hear lest we let them get away from us in this manner. (Heb. 2:1)

5 Paul declared that we should not be weary in well what? (2 Thes. 3:13)

7 Paul taught that we should not let the sun go down upon this descriptive word for our anger. (Eph. 4:26)

9 Paul admonished the Romans that they should overcome evil with this attribute. (Rom. 12:21)

10 Jesus said that this member of the Godhead would not come to the Apostles unless He left. (John 16:7)

11 Paul told the Corinthians that he could not speak spiritual things, but must speak carnal things because they were not adults, but these. (1 Cor. 3:1)

12 Paul said all who live godly in Christ Jesus will suffer this. (2 Tim. 3:12)

14 Paul declares that we should, "Owe no man any _____ , but love one another." (Rom. 13:8)

16 James states that we should confess these personal flaws to each other. (James 5:16)

17 Jesus told Jairus that he should tell how many people about the raising of his daughter. (Mark 5:43)

18 Paul said that the infirmities of the weak should be borne by those who are this. (Rom. 15:1)

20 Paul told the Thessalonians that we are to rejoice for this unending period. (1 Thes. 5:16)

21 Paul exhorted the Thessalonians not to quench this eternal part of man. (1 Thes. 5:19)

22 Paul said that to be carnally minded is this. (Rom. 8:6)

24 Jesus said that those that were not against Him were on His what? (Mark 9:40)

26 Paul advised that we should not let our good be spoken of as this. (Rom. 14:16)

29 Paul exhorted the Thessalonians to be patient toward how many men? (1 Thes. 5:14)

581. According to Peter, there is forever reserved for the wicked a mist of what? (2 Pet. 2:17)

582. After the ascension of Jesus and after the arrest of the Apostles, how did the council punish the Apostles for teaching Christ? (Acts 5:40–41)

583. Paul declared he had received "stripes" by the Jews, how many times? (2 Cor. 11:24)

584. Paul said that he bore in his body, the what of the Lord Jesus? (Gal. 6:17)

585. What were the Apostles to do when they were rejected by a household or community? (Matt. 10:14)

586. Paul was punished with what in Thyatira? (Acts 16:14, 23)

587. Paul said that everyone is cursed that hangeth on a what? (Gal. 3:13)

588. What Apostle was beaten for polluting the temple with a Greek? (Acts 21:28, 32)

589. If the children of the kingdom are not righteous, they may be cast out to where? (Matt. 8:12)

590. No murderer has what, according to John? (1 John 3:15)

591. John records that no man spoke openly of Jesus for fear of whom? (John 7:13)

592. What object that gave evidence of fruit, but had none, did Jesus curse for hypocrisy? (Matt. 21:19)

593. Paul cursed Barjesus the sorcerer with what? (Acts 13:6–11)

594. If you blaspheme against what person, it is not forgiven? (Matt. 12:31)

595. According to Paul, Moses' generation could not enter the promised land because of what? (Heb. 3:19)

596. Paul declared that the last enemy Jesus would destroy is what? (1 Cor. 15:26)

597. In the parable of the ten virgins, who came while the foolish virgins were out buying oil? (Matt. 25:10)

598. Paul said if we defile our what, God will destroy us? (1 Cor. 3:17)

True or False?

1270. We are warned that there is a beam in our eye that prevents us from seeing a brother's mote. (Matt. 7:5)

Match the questions on the left with the answers on the right.
The solution is on page 298.

A. This was the sin of the woman taken
    to Jesus in an attempt to entrap Him.
    (John 8:3)

Satan

B. According to John, he that denies
    the Father and the Son is called this.
    (1 John 2:22)

Good

C. This was the sin of the Galatians
    (modern term). (Gal. 1:6)

Willfully

D. Who had filled the heart of Ananias'
    to conspire over the price of the prop-
    erty. (Acts 5:3)

Law

E. If you know to do _____, and
    you do it not, it is sin. (James 4:17)

The AntiChrist

F. Peter said that this virtue would over-
    come a multitude of sins. (1 Pet. 4:8)

Nicolatians

G. The sacrifice of Jesus for sins does
    not protect us if we sin in this manner.
    (Heb. 10:26)

Adultery

H. If we say we have no sin, we only do
    this to ourselves. (1 John 1:8)

Charity

I. The church at Ephesus hated the sins
    of this group. (Rev. 2:1, 6)

Deceive

J. If you sin according to the law, you
    shall be judged according to this.
    (Rom. 2:12)

Apostasy

599. Paul taught that blood sacrifices of what animals would not take away sins? (Heb. 10:4)

600. How did Paul say "Saul's" sins were committed so that he obtained mercy? (1 Tim. 1:13)

601. With regard to the woman taken in adultery, what did Jesus not do to her? (John 8:11)

602. Paul states that we only know sin because of the what? (Rom. 7:7)

603. Paul said because of sin, what event "passed" on all men? (Rom. 5:12)

604. Paul said that the wages of sin are what? (Rom. 6:23)

605. Jesus proved to the rulers He could forgive sins by healing what person? (Matt. 9:6)

606. Paul taught that when we are servants of sin, we are free from all what? (Rom. 6:20)

607. The disciples asked if either of whom had sinned, to cause a certain man to be born blind? (John 9:2)

608. According to Paul, the strength of sin is the what? (1 Cor. 15:56)

SIN WORD SEARCH
Rules And Results

Solution on page 300

```
U  N  R  I  G  H  T  E  O  U  S  N  E  S  S
B  K  G  T  H  K  M  L  A  W  B  N  Q  M  F
L  N  C  M  G  R  G  W  R  C  J  K  S  N  K
M  K  H  J  C  X  R  N  A  C  H  S  F  G  B
V  V  D  N  M  D  A  R  X  N  E  U  L  R  K
T  K  R  T  M  D  C  D  Y  N  O  T  R  L  D
M  K  W  R  J  L  E  W  S  R  Q  T  L  C  M
V  K  Y  U  C  H  H  U  O  L  R  R  H  R  H
M  B  T  T  K  K  O  T  R  G  H  T  G  E  L
Y  R  T  H  M  E  A  N  N  T  M  L  G  N  R
Y  K  T  Y  T  I  N  R  A  T  K  T  P  K  Y
L  G  G  H  D  D  H  E  K  G  Q  Z  W  Z  C
H  D  G  E  R  N  D  L  Q  D  V  Z  Q  D  J
X  I  M  Y  R  Y  L  T  N  L  T  T  N  F  N
R  K  V  R  C  L  O  A  K  K  K  L  N  J  R
```

- Paul taught that we should sin not, but awake to our what? (1 Cor. 15:34)

- John defines sin as the transgression of this. (1 John 3:4)

- In Romans, Paul condemned men for burning in their lusts one toward whom? (Rom. 1:27)

- If we say we have no sin we deceive ourselves, and this virtue is not in us. (1 John 1:8)

- John states that all unrighteousness is sin: and there is a sin NOT unto this. (1 John 5:17)

- Because Jesus came, the Jews no longer had one of these to cover their sins. (John 15:22)

- The last organization you should consult when resolving sins between individuals is this. (Matt. 18:15–17)

- Paul states that sin cannot have dominion over us because we are not under the law, but under this. (Rom. 6:14)

- John declares that all this is sin. (1 John 5:17)

- Paul taught that Jesus purged our sins and became this with the Father. (Heb. 9:14–15)

609. Who did Ananias lie to concerning the price of his property? (Acts 5:3)

610. If you lie and say you are Jews and are not, you are of whose Synagogue? (Rev. 3:9)

611. What did Sapphira and Ananias conspire about? (Acts 5:1–3)

612. Paul taught that latter-day apostates will speak lies in what? (1 Tim. 4:2)

613. What did the Rulers of the Jews gave to the soldiers guarding Jesus' tomb to get them to tell a lie? (Matt. 28:12)

Trick Question

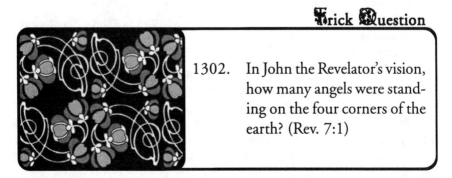

1302. In John the Revelator's vision, how many angels were standing on the four corners of the earth? (Rev. 7:1)

SATAN AND POSSESSION
Rules And Results

Solution on page 294

Across

3 Paul taught that Satan's ministers can be transformed, as if they were ministers of this. (2 Cor. 11:15)

7 Mary Magdalene had seven of these evil spirits cast out of her. (Mark 16:9)

8 Paul states that it was not Adam who was deceived, but this person. (1 Tim. 2:14)

9 These kinds of bonds could not hold the demonic whose name was Legion. (Mark 5:3)

13 Paul delivers Hymengeus and this man to Satan in his first letter to Timothy. (1 Tim. 1:20)

14 The devil disguised Christ's first temptation in the wilderness by asking Him to turn stones into this food staple. (Matt. 4:3)

16 After being bound for one thousand years, Satan will be loosed for this little period. (Rev. 20:3)

20 Jesus referred to the devil as the _____ of this world. (John 14:30)

23 After the little season the devil is finally cast into this geological feature of fire and brimstone? (Rev. 20:3, 10)

24 Jesus told Satan that man should live by every _____ that comes from the mouth of God. (Matt. 4:4)

25 James said that if we resist the devil, he will do this from us. (James 4:7)

26 The seven sons of Sceva adjured evil spirits in the name of this Deity. (Acts 19:13–14)

Down

1 When the Lord comes again, Satan will be bound for a thousand what? (Rev. 20:2)

2 This is the name of the prince of devils. (Matt. 12:24)

4 The devils in the Gadarene possession requested that they be allowed to go into these animals. (Matt. 8:31)

5 The demonic named Legion who lived in the tombs, cut himself with these. (Mark 5:5)

6 This was the name of the demonic that possessed the man in the country of the Gadarenes. (Mark 5:9)

10 The Gadarene devils saluted Jesus as the Son of this supreme Deity. (Matt. 8:29)

11 Paul said he had a thorn in this as a constant messenger from Satan to buffet him. (2 Cor. 12:7)

12 This kind of evil spirit (found in the lunatic child), can be cast out only by fasting and this. (Matt. 17:21)

15 This is what John called false Christs in his first epistle. (1 John 2:18)

17 The seven sons of this man tried and failed to exorcize evil spirits. (Acts 19:14)

18 Jesus told the disciples that they could not heal the lunatic child because of this lack of faith. (Matt. 17:20)

19 At the conclusion of His third temptation in the wilderness, Jesus commanded Satan: "Get thee _____." (Matt. 4:10)

21 Jesus cautioned that when an unclean spirit is cast out and finds the house clean and swept, he gathers this number of unclean spirits and reenters that house. (Matt. 12:45)

22 According to Matthew, this is the number of men that were possessed and lived in the Gergesenes tombs. (Matt. 8:28)

True or False?

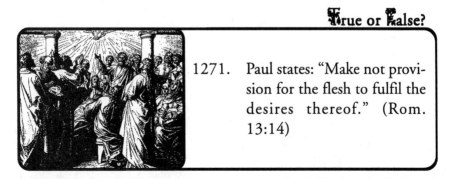

1271. Paul states: "Make not provision for the flesh to fulfil the desires thereof." (Rom. 13:14)

The Gospel In Action

V

614. What is Jesus' discourse in Matthew, Chapters 5, 6, and 7 called?

615. What was the immediate result of Jesus' bread of life sermon? (John 6:66)

616. What is the chapter in John that contains the "light of the world" sermon?

617. At the time of the bread of life sermon, Jesus declared that one of the twelve would betray Him and was a what? (John 6:70–71)

618. What is the name of the sermon contained in John 10?

619. At the Last Supper, who asked Jesus how it was that He would manifest Himself to the Apostles, but not to the world? (John 14:22)

620. Jesus taught the bread of life sermon in what city? (John 6:59)

621. What was the reaction of the multitude to the discourse Peter gave at Pentecost? (Acts 2:37)

622. What is the book and chapter reference for the bread of life sermon?

Match the questions on the left with the answers on the right.
The solution is on page 281.

A. Paul said the gospel is the power of God unto this. (Rom. 1:16)

Lilies

B. Where two or three are gathered in His name, this person is there. (Matt. 18:20)

Predestinate

C. The gospel of the circumcision was committed to this Apostle. (Gal. 2:7)

Meat

D. Labor not for that item which parishes, but for that item which endures. (John 6:27)

Faith

E. James said the trying of this, works patience. (James 1:3)

Salvation

F. Being hearers of the word only and not doers, deceives only this person. (James 1:22)

Yourself

G. Paul said, whom God did foreknow, He did also this. (Rom. 8:29)

Christ

H. Jesus compared the greatest in the kingdom to this small infant. (Matt. 18:4)

Truth

I. Solomon in all his glory was not as one of these. (Matt. 6:28–29)

Peter

J. Jesus said that if we know this, it will make us free. (John 8:32)

Child

623. By what method did Paul say he received the gospel? (Gal. 1:12)

624. The Jews rejected the gospel, so Paul turned to whom? (Acts 13:46)

625. According to James, pure religion is to visit the widow and whom? (James 1:27)

626. What group did Peter tell the Apostles in Judea had also received the gospel? (Acts 11:1)

627. The gospel was preached to the dead so that they could be what, according to men in the flesh? (1 Pet. 4:6)

628. What two Apostles were sent to Samaria after they heard its people had received the gospel? (Acts 8:14)

629. Whether Paul or what, preach any other gospel to you, let them be accursed? (Gal. 1:8)

630. The gospel of circumcision was committed to Peter, the gospel of uncircumcision was committed to whom? (Gal. 2:7)

631. The gospel was preached to the ancients, but was not mixed with what? (Heb. 4:2)

632. Paul said that if we receive the Gospel and reject it, what do we do to Jesus anew? (Heb. 6:6)

633. Paul said that accepting the Gospel and then leaving it puts Jesus to open what? (Heb. 6:6)

634. According to the Beatitudes, blessed are the poor in spirit for theirs is what? (Matt. 5:3)

635. In the Beatitudes; blessed are they that mourn for they receive what? (Matt. 5:4)

636. In the Beatitudes; blessed are the meek for they shall receive what? (Matt. 5:5)

637. According to the Beatitudes, blessed are they who hunger and thirst after righteousness, for they shall be what? (Matt. 5:6)

638. The Beatitudes states, blessed are the merciful for they shall receive what? (Matt. 5:7)

639. What do the "blessed" that are the pure in heart receive? (Matt. 5:8)

640. According to the Beatitudes, blessed are the peacemakers, for they will be called what? (Matt. 5:9)

641. In the Beatitudes, blessed are they who are persecuted for righteousness sake, for they will receive what? (Matt. 5:10)

642. According to the Beatitudes, blessed are they who are reviled and persecuted, for who were persecuted before them? (Matt. 5:11–12)

643. In the Beatitudes, which "blessed" see God? (Matt. 5:8)

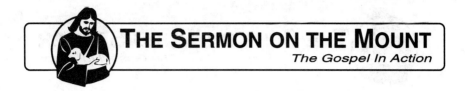

644. What should you do to people who hate you? (Matt. 5:44)

645. According to the Sermon on the Mount, repeating what name twice does not guarantee that you will attain heaven? (Matt. 7:21)

646. According to the Sermon on the Mount, when men see our good works, who is glorified? (Matt. 5:16)

647. In the Sermon on the Mount; which "blessed" shall be comforted? (Matt. 5:4)

648. In the Sermon on the Mount, what neither toil nor spin, yet grow? (Matt. 6:28)

649. In the Beatitudes, which "blessed" are filled? (Matt. 5:6)

650. What is located in Matthew 7:12 (common name)?

651. How did the people react to the Sermon on Mount? (Matt. 7:28)

652. In the Sermon on the Mount, the Lord said that God sends the rain upon whom? (Matt. 5:45)

THE SERMON WORD SEARCH
The Gospel In Action

Solution on page 297

```
T  L  M  B  O  R  R  O  W  E  B  N  N  T
E  Y  E  W  H  T  K  V  R  H  O  F  I  K
M  P  O  O  R  N  P  U  H  I  X  U  L  L
N  S  B  P  Y  N  S  Y  T  D  R  G  L  Z
L  M  T  Y  T  A  J  A  N  F  T  M  B  B
T  M  N  R  E  N  C  N  G  T  C  B  F  E
T  X  O  R  E  I  K  T  K  M  U  P  L  A
U  M  T  U  N  E  K  N  Y  G  T  U  X  T
R  K  H  R  R  H  T  S  R  N  F  Y  S  I
N  J  O  P  Q  N  O  S  I  I  T  B  P  T
O  F  P  J  R  R  Y  A  C  K  L  N  I  U
Z  U  K  N  P  F  L  R  X  X  P  H  R  D
Y  T  T  E  Q  P  E  N  T  D  G  C  I  E
Y  K  L  M  Y  M  B  X  L  K  M  X  T  S
```

- In the Beatitudes, these blessed obtain mercy. (Matt. 5:7)

  (a) spiritual
  (b) poor
  (c) merciful

- Jesus taught that you should not turn away those who would do this from you. (Matt. 5:42)

  (a) work
  (b) help
  (c) borrow

- If your right eye offends you, you should pluck it this way. (Matt. 5:29)

  (a) out
  (b) off
  (c) away

- If you are smitten on the right cheek, this is what you should do with the other. (Matt. 5:39)

  (a) spare
  (b) turn
  (c) protect

- Good trees cannot bring forth this evil item. (Matt. 7:18)

  (a) leaves
  (b) branches
  (c) fruit

- The beam we should first remove is located in our what? (Matt. 7:3)

  (a) chest
  (b) mouth
  (c) eye

- The blessed that are comforted are those that do this. (Matt. 5:4)

  (a) cry
  (b) mourn
  (c) pray

- The blessed that receive the kingdom of heaven are those that are poor in this. (Matt. 5:3)

  (a) money
  (b) spirit
  (c) health

- Luke states that the material taught in the Sermon on the Mount was delivered on this. (Luke 6:17)

  (a) mountain
  (b) lake
  (c) plain

- The first blessed are those that are lacking in this in spirit. (Matt. 5:3)

  (a) weak
  (b) happy
  (c) poor

- The Lord states that hypocrites pray in the synagogues and in these. (Matt. 6:5)

  (a) fields
  (b) houses
  (c) streets

- If your hand offends you, you should do this to remove it. (Matt. 5:30)

  (a) rub
  (b) cut
  (c) chop

- Jesus said the only reason that justified putting away a wife was this. (Matt. 5:32)

  (a) adultery
  (b) fornication
  (c) murder

- The conditions of blessedness described in the Sermon on the Mount are called these.

  (a) beatitudes
  (b) thankfulness
  (c) blessings

- Where this is, your heart will be also. (Matt. 6:21)

  (a) heart
  (b) money
  (c) treasure

- When the Sermon on the Mount completed, Jesus came down from the mountain and healed a man of this. (Matt. 8:2)

  (a) blindness
  (b) leprosy
  (c) palsy

THE SERMON CROSSWORD
The Gospel In Action

Solution on page 296

Across

1   Destruction's way is described as being what? (Matt. 7:13)

6   Who did Jesus declare breaks through and steals our treasures? (Matt. 6:19)

7　How many masters you cannot serve at the same time? (Matt. 6:24)

8　We are to let our light do this before men. (Matt. 5:16)

9　How many miles should you go if you are compelled to go one. (Matt. 5:41)

12　Before we can cast out the mote from our brother's eye we should cast out a what from our own eye? (Matt. 7:5)

13　What are you in danger of if you call someone a fool? (Matt. 5:22)

15　What is good for nothing if it loses its savor? (Matt. 5:13)

18　The Lord declared that the body is more than this covering. (Matt. 6:25)

19　Jesus taught as one having authority and not as these. (Matt. 7:29)

20　The "blessed" who hunger and thirst after righteousness are what? (Matt. 5:6)

22　We are instructed to not cast pearls before what animal? (Matt. 7:6)

24　Corrupt trees cannot bring forth this kind of fruit. (Matt. 7:18)

26　If you are sued at the law and lose the coat, you should give this also. (Matt. 5:40)

27　The Apostles were commanded to be a what to the world? (Matt. 5:16)

28　Men do not light candles to put them under these containers. (Matt. 5:15)

29　We should give our alms not publically, but in this manner. (Matt. 6:4)

31　God will forgive ours if we forgive men theirs. (Matt. 6:14)

33　You are in danger of hellfire if you call someone this. (Matt. 5:22)

35　We are to beware of false prophets who are inwardly what type of ravening animals? (Matt. 7:15)

38　Our light is to shine before men so that they may see our good what? (Matt. 5:16)

39　We pray to be delivered from this. (Matt. 6:13)

41　Moths and this reddish substance corrupt treasures that are laid up in the earth. (Matt. 6:19)

42　Christ declared that He did not come to destroy the law but to do this (alternate spelling). (Matt. 5:17)

44　How many find the strait and narrow way to eternal life? (Matt. 7:14)

45　The blessed that will inherit the earth are these. (Matt. 5:5)

46　What emotion should you show to your enemies? (Matt. 5:44)

47　Christ taught as one having this, and not as the scribes. (Matt. 7:29)

53　The Father makes what orb rise upon both the evil and the good? (Matt. 5:45)

54　What should we not cast before swine? (Matt. 7:6)

56　This is what you should leave at the temple altar until you are reconciled with a brother. (Matt. 5:23–24)

57　You cannot add one of these to your stature? (Matt. 6:27)

59　When the winds and rain came, the house which was built upon sand did what? (Matt. 7:27)

61　Blessed are they that mourn for they receive what? (Matt. 5:4)

62　If this is set upon a hill, it cannot be hid. (Matt. 5:14)

Down

2　What do hypocrites do to their faces to appear to men that they are fasting? (Matt. 6:16)

3   Swear not by your head because you cannot make one hair black or what? (Matt. 5:36)

4   Let not the left hand know what this hand is doing when giving alms. (Matt. 6:3)

5   What does Matthew 5:48 command us to be?

7   What we should not lay up for ourselves on the earth? (Matt. 6:19)

10   Salt that has lost its savor is good for what? (Matt. 5:13)

11   We are to "knock" so that it may be what? (Matt. 7:7)

14   Doing secret alms produces open what from God? (Matt. 6:4)

16   Jesus said that even these people loved those who loved them. (Matt. 5:46)

17   Destruction's gate is described as what size? (Matt. 7:13)

20   Swear not by the earth, for it is God's what? (Matt. 5:35)

21   Do not give holy things to what animal? (Matt. 7:6)

23   We are to "ask," so that answers can be what? (Matt. 7:7)

25   In the Lord's prayer, God forgives our debts as we forgive our what? (Matt. 6:12)

26   The Lord told us to bless them that do what to us? (Matt. 5:44)

28   In the Lord's prayer, we ask God to give us this daily food. (Matt. 6:11)

30   When praying in secret, we should enter into one of these. (Matt. 6:6)

32   When fasting, Jesus said that we should do this to our head. (Matt. 6:17)

34   We are to take no thought for what day after today? (Matt. 6:34)

36   We should not use this kind of repetitions when praying. (Matt. 6:7)

37   The foolish man built his house upon what substance? (Matt. 7:26)

40   We should not give that which is what to the dogs? (Matt. 7:6)

42   Hewn down trees with evil fruit are cast into what element? (Matt. 7:19)

43   You know false prophets by their what? (Matt. 7:16)

44   We are to "seek" so that we may what? (Matt. 7:7)

45   Because of the beam in our own eye, we cannot see this to cast from our brother's eye. (Matt. 7:5)

47   Jesus declared that these men were the salt of the earth. (Matt. 5:13)

48   You are in danger of the council if you speak this word. (Matt. 5:22)

49   In the Lord's prayer, we pray not to be lead into this. (Matt. 6:13)

50   Hypocrites disfigured their faces so people will know they are doing this? (Matt. 6:16)

51   "Thou shalt not kill" was expanded so that you could not even be _____ with a brother. (Matt. 5:22)

52   "Is not the life more than" this protein? (Matt. 6:25)

55   The wise man built his house upon this to avoid the elements. (Matt. 7:24)

58   Swear not by your head because you cannot make one hair white or what? (Matt. 5:36)

60   You commit adultery in the heart if you look upon a women and feel this emotion. (Matt. 5:28)

653. In what chapter of 1 Corinthians does Paul write about the gift of tongues?

654. How many "understood words," did Paul teach were better than ten thousand words in an unknown tongue? (1 Cor. 14:19)

655. Paul said that Timothy's "gift" had been given him by revelation, through what method? (1 Tim. 4:14)

656. Who did Jesus praise for casting two mites into the treasury? (Mark 12:42–44)

657. Paul said that speaking in an unknown tongue only edifies what person? (1 Cor. 14:4)

658. There is the gift of tongues and conversely the gift of what? (1 Cor. 12:10)

659. Paul taught that he who does what, is greater than one speaking in tongues without an interpreter? (1 Cor. 14:5)

660. Cornelius' household exercised what gift of the Spirit? (Acts 10:46)

661. 1 Corinthians, chapter 12 deals with the diversity of what gifts?

662. What were the three gifts the wise men presented to the baby Jesus? (Matt. 2:11)

663. Who was the Apostle to whom Jesus first gave a sop at the Last Supper? (John 13:26)

664. What does Paul declare is the gift of God through Jesus Christ? (Rom. 6:23)

665. When Jesus cleansed the temple, the reaction of the Jews was to ask Him for a what? (John 2:18)

666. What was the nationality of the man Paul was accused of taking with him into the temple, thus polluting it? (Acts 21:28)

667. What did Jesus do for the second time at the temple after His final entry into Jerusalem? (Matt. 21:12)

668. At the death of Jesus, what item in the temple was rent from top to bottom? (Matt. 27:51)

669. Paul said that our bodies are the temple of whom? (1 Cor. 6:19)

670. What did Jesus use to drive the money changers from the temple? (John 2:15)

671. What man testified to the baby Jesus' divinity at the temple? (Luke 2:25)

672. What "temple" did Jesus refer to when He said He would destroy the temple and raise it again in three days? (John 2:21)

673. What did Jesus say the money changers had made of His temple? (Matt. 21:13)

674. What did Jesus overthrow when He first cleansed the temple? (John 2:15)

675. What age was Jesus when He was found teaching in the temple as a boy? (Luke 2:42, 46)

676. What punishment did Paul suffer for taking a Greek into the temple? (Acts 21:28, 32)

677. What was Christ's prophecy concerning the temple? (Matt. 24:1–2)

True or False?

1272.   John declared that whosoever commits sin, also transgresses the law. (1 John 3:4)

MIRACLES WORD SEARCH
The Gospel In Action

Solution on page 290

```
O  N  E  B  O  R  N  B  L  I  N  D  P  S
D  S  E  A  M  V  Z  D  R  X  K  T  L  F
C  Q  E  Y  E  S  L  L  D  Q  N  I  N  N
P  K  C  L  K  H  Q  M  H  E  V  L  S  K
N  V  Z  N  T  Q  H  T  K  E  A  U  L  L
S  P  C  R  R  B  A  V  D  T  E  D  T  P
C  T  G  X  C  B  E  F  X  A  T  J  O  E
O  S  H  K  B  B  O  E  M  K  F  W  U  T
R  K  I  A  L  E  W  I  L  R  N  K  C  E
N  J  S  T  C  B  T  Q  R  Z  D  C  H  R
T  K  K  N  D  R  J  J  G  B  E  Y  E  Q
W  Q  I  W  A  O  F  G  T  M  F  B  D  J
H  R  R  B  L  K  W  J  Y  P  L  U  D
P  N  L  R  R  R  F  N  G  L  K  Z  N  B
```

- The Pharisees accused Jesus of casting out devils by this. (Matt. 9:34)

  (a) spirit
  (b) prince of the air
  (c) prince of devils

- To calm the tempest, Jesus rebuked the wind and this. (Matt. 8:26)

  (a) sea
  (b) waves
  (c) storm

- Jesus anointed the eyes of this person with clay and told him to wash in a pool to receive his sight. (John 9:1, 6–7)

  (a) one born blind
  (b) the blind at Jericho
  (c) the blind beggar

- Jesus was accused by the Pharisees of performing miracles by the power of this person. (Matt. 12:24)

  (a) the Spirit
  (b) the devil
  (c) Beelzebub

- When Jesus said Jairus' daughter

only "sleepeth," the mourners laughed Him to this. (Matt. 9:24)

(a) scorn
(b) embarrassment
(c) shame

• The impotent man by the pool at Bethesda was healed on this day of the week. (John 5:10)

(a) the second
(b) sabbath
(c) holy day

• Before the feeding of the five thousand, Jesus instructed the Apostles to tell the men in the multitude to do this. (John 6:10)

(a) line up
(b) bring children first
(c) sit down

• The name of the disciple who walked with Jesus upon the water is this. (Matt. 14:28–29)

(a) John
(b) Matthew
(c) Peter

• The only recorded miracle performed at Jericho was the healing of this blind man. (Mark 10:46)

(a) Bill
(b) Bartimaeus
(c) Judas

• To heal the blind men as He left Jericho, Jesus touched this part of them. (Matt. 20:34)

(a) mouths
(b) hair
(c) eyes

• Paul performed a miracle by raising a boy named Eutychus from this. (Acts 20:9–10)

(a) grave
(b) bed
(c) dead

• The woman with an issue of blood did this to the hem of Christ's garment to be healed. (Matt. 9:20, 22)

(a) touched
(b) ironed
(c) washed

🎩rick 🎩uestion

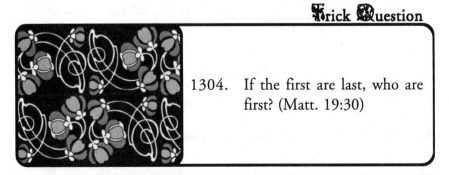

1304. If the first are last, who are first? (Matt. 19:30)

678. What was the unique method used to heal the nobleman's son? (John 4:50)

679. What did Peter have none of to give, before he healed the lame man? (Acts 3:6)

680. What would be a logical name for the miracle involving Christ's tribute tax money? (Matt. 17:27)

681. What is the miracle the nine "disciples" (Apostles) could not perform? (Matt. 17:15–16)

682. What was the miracle Jesus performed at the Sea of Tiberias after the resurrection? (John 21:6)

683. In the circumstances surrounding the healing of the nobleman's son, what did the nobleman ask Jesus to do? (John 4:49)

684. The man with the dropsy was healed by Jesus on what day? (Luke 14:1–2)

685. What happened to those who touched the hem of Jesus' garment? (Matt. 14:36)

686. Jesus asked the man born blind if he believed on what Deity? (John 9:35–36)

687. Tabitha was raised from the dead by which Apostle? (Acts 9:40)

688. What was the question Jesus put to the impotent man by the pool of Bethesda? (John 5:6)

689. What miracle was performed at the call of Peter and Andrew to follow Jesus? (Luke 5:6)

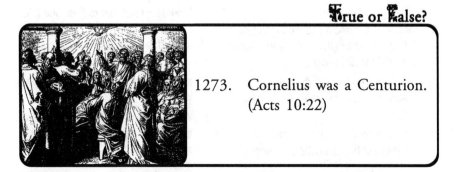

1273.   Cornelius was a Centurion. (Acts 10:22)

MIRACLES CROSSWORD
The Gospel In Action

Solution on page 289

Across

3   To get to Jesus in the house, the one sick with the palsy was lowered through the what? (Mark 2:4)

6   The age of the lame man healed by Peter was above how many years? (Acts 4:22)

8   Jesus performed a healing in stages. What was the malady of the inflicted man? (Mark 8:23–25)

11 Jesus touched what forbidden and un-clean man to heal him? (Mark 1:40–41)

12 This left Jesus when the women with an issue of blood touched the hem of His garment and was healed. (Mark 5:30)

13 The man lowered from the housetop on a stretcher to be healed was sick with the what? (Luke 5:18–19)

14 Mark recorded that to heal one blind man, Jesus put what unique liquid into the man's eyes? (Mark 8:23)

15 The blind man that Jesus healed in stages first saw men as what plants walking? (Mark 8:24)

16 When Jesus and Peter entered the ship after walking on the water, what stopped? (Matt. 14:32)

17   Jesus raised whose daughter from the dead? (Mark 5:22–23)

21   What the high priest and those with him were filled with as a result of the miracles of the Apostles? (Acts 5:17)

Down

1   How many blind men were healed immediately after the raising of Jairus' daughter? (Matt. 9:27, 30)

2   At the raising of the widow's son, Jesus touched what item that made the procession stop? (Luke 7:14)

4   How many loaves were available at the feeding of the five thousand? (Matt. 14:17)

5   On what day of the week did Christ heal the man with a withered hand? (Matt. 12:10, 13)

6   Paul's first healing was a man who was crippled in his what? (Acts 14:8, 10)

7   How many blind men does Matthew record were healed as Jesus departed from Jericho? (Matt. 20:29–30, 34)

9   Jesus told Jairus his daughter was not dead, but was only what? (Matt. 9:24)

10   Before healing the one sick with the palsy, Jesus forgave his what? (Matt. 9:2)

13   Who healed AEneas of the palsy? (Acts 9:34)

18   The man born blind was told to wash his eyes in what pool to complete the healing? (John 9:7)

19   Of the ten lepers healed, how many gave thanks and glorified God? (Luke 17:15)

20   The impotent man at the Bethesda pool said he did not have a what to help him? (John 5:7)

Trick Question

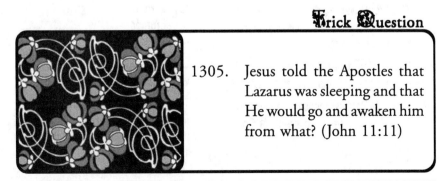

1305.   Jesus told the Apostles that Lazarus was sleeping and that He would go and awaken him from what? (John 11:11)

FOOD AND DRINK
The Gospel In Action

Solution on page 280

```
M  T  T  D  P  S  H  E  W  B  R  E  A  D
I  Y  T  Y  R  Y  F  F  K  K  T  H  M  N
L  R  M  W  C  I  W  N  Q  T  C  G  Z  M
K  Z  X  Q  E  E  N  W  O  A  W  M  R  R
C  G  Y  M  R  L  R  K  M  N  E  O  D  P
A  Q  T  D  W  Z  V  O  T  F  E  P  B  R
P  G  N  L  C  A  T  E  I  L  R  H  Y  A
E  A  L  T  M  S  T  L  F  B  Q  Y  B  Y
R  Z  R  K  V  I  N  E  G  A  R  S  G  E
N  Q  M  T  N  J  P  N  R  K  B  I  A  R
A  B  A  R  L  E  Y  D  V  M  D  C  F  H
U  E  K  X  S  I  X  B  U  A  H  I  E  G
M  D  J  E  S  U  S  R  L  F  J  A  W  R
J  Q  B  X  B  Y  C  A  N  T  P  N  M  L
```

- This Apostle told Jesus of the meager amount of food available before the feeding of the five thousand. (John 6:8–9)

- The bread was made of this grain at the feeding of the five thousand. (John 6:13)

- Paul declared that the kingdom of God is not meat and this. (Rom. 14:17)

- What did Paul symbolically feed to the Corinthians rather than meat? (1 Cor. 3:2)

- The Syrophenician woman answered the Lord by stating that from their master's table, the dogs eat these. (Matt. 15:27)

  (a) scraps
  (b) crumbs
  (c) left overs

- Christ was given this to drink while He was on the cross. (Matt. 27:48)

- This number of baskets filled with fragments of food were left over at the feeding of the five thousand. (Matt. 14:20)

- How many fishes were available to feed the four thousand? (Matt. 15:34)

- Paul advised Timothy to drink a little wine for the sake of this internal organ. (1 Tim. 5:23)

- The true bread from heaven was not manna, but who? (John 6:57–58)

- In the parable of the marriage supper, how many of the guests originally invited to the supper were allowed to eat? (Luke 14:24)

- This is the city Jesus went to after the feeding of the five thousand. (John 6:24)

- In the synagogue at Capernaum, Jesus declared Himself to be the bread of this. (John 6:35)

- Jesus declared that King David ate this unlawful food and yet was justified. (Matt. 12:4)

- This is the number of fishes that were available at the feeding of the five thousand. (Matt. 14:17)

- Paul stated that every creature is sanctified by God for food, and is to be received with thanksgiving and this. (1 Tim. 1:4–5)

- Who had the five loaves and two fishes at the feeding of the five thousand? (John 6:9)

- This is the number of water pots that were filled with wine by Jesus' miracle. (John 2:6)

- Jesus ate with publicans and sinners because He said they who are whole do not need a _____. (Matt. 9:12)

- This is what Jesus turned to wine. (John 2:9)

- Paul said that the Hebrews had need of milk, and not strong what? (Heb. 5:12)
  - (a) food
  - (b) drink
  - (c) meat

True or False?

1274. According to James, we should count it joy to endure temptation. (James 1:12)

690. What does Luke say Jesus ate as a sign of His resurrection? (Luke 24:42–43)

691. What sin did the scribes and Pharisees accuse Jesus' disciples of when they were eating bread? (Matt. 15:2)

692. The disciples marveled when the cursed fig tree did what? (Matt. 21:20)

693. In excess of what amount of bread did Philip say would be needed, to feed five thousand people even "a little"? (John 6:7)

694. Which feast of the Jews was near at the feeding of the five thousand? (John 6:4)

695. Paul said that he that used milk was unskillful in the word of what, for he is a babe? (Heb. 5:13)

696. The feast of unleavened bread is also called what? (Luke 22:1)

697. What must we symbolically "drink" of the Son of man? (John 6:53)

698. What question did John's disciples ask Jesus concerning food? (Matt. 9:14)

699. What did Jesus tell us to seek before we seek earthly riches? (Matt. 6:33)

700. Paul said that the love of money was the root of all what? (1 Tim. 6:10)

701. Paul taught that after leaving the faith, some seek money after piercing themselves with many what? (1 Tim. 6:10)

702. Which Apostle pledged the tribute money for Jesus? (Matt. 17:24–25)

703. Paul warned that they that are rich fall into many foolish and hurtful what? (1 Tim. 6:9)

704. Where was the coin found that paid the temple tribute tax for Jesus and Peter? (Matt. 17:27)

705. Luke records that Jesus said if you could not be faithful with unrighteous mammon, who will commit to your trust the true what? (Luke 16:11)

706. What did Paul say was the "amount" that we can carry out of this world? (1 Tim. 6:7)

707. Jesus told the rich man that to be perfect, he should go and do what, and then follow Him? (Matt. 19:21)

708. What did Jesus' disciples ask Him after hearing how hard it was for the rich to get into heaven? (Matt. 19:25)

709. In the parable of the pounds, how many pounds were given to each servant? (Luke 19:13)

710. What amount did the widow cast into the treasury? (Mark 12:42)

711. What chapter in James warns the rich?

712. Before the feeding of the five thousand, which Apostle answered Jesus that two hundred pennyworth was not enough to feed the multitude a little? (John 6:7)

713. The fate of the parabolic unmerciful servant was to be delivered to whom, until his debt was paid? (Matt. 18:34)

714. What did the Jewish rulers buy with the thirty pieces of silver Judas returned to them? (Matt. 27:7)

715. What type of coin was used as the example when Jesus was asked if it was lawful to pay tribute to Caesar? (Matt. 22:19)

716. James warned us that even the _____ also believed and trembled. (James 2:19)

717. Paul said that we should mark and avoid those who cause _____ and _____. (Rom. 16:17)

718. Paul warned us to refuse profane and old wives _____. (1 Tim. 4:7)

719. Paul admonished the Corinthians to put away from them wicked persons who were without _____. (1 Cor. 5:13)

720. Jesus warned that in the last days, if any say, "Lo, here is Christ" we should believe it _____. (Matt. 24:23)

721. John declares that we should "try" the _____. (1 John 4:1)

722. The wise men asked _____ ___ _____ to help locate the newborn king of the Jews. (Matt. 2:1–2)

723. Jesus told Nicodemus that a man must be what, to gain the kingdom? (John 3:3)

724. Peter warned the people that there were false prophets and false _____ among them who would bring heresies, even denying the Lord. (2 Pet. 2:1)

725. Paul cautioned Timothy to avoid babblings and oppositions of _____, falsely so called. (1 Tim. 6:20)

726. After healing the leper, Jesus told him to show himself to the _____. (Matt. 8:3–4)

727. Paul warned the Thessalonians concerning those who walked among them _____. (2 Thes. 3:6)

728. Paul praised the Colossians for the love they had toward all what? (Col. 1:4)

729. What did Paul say can separate us from the love of Christ? (Rom. 8:35–39)

730. Paul taught that God loveth a cheerful what? (2 Cor. 9:7)

731. If we love what, the love of the Father is not in us? (1 John 2:15)

732. Paul said that the love of what, is the root of all evil? (1 Tim. 6:10)

733. Paul said it was written that God loved Jacob, but hated whom? (Rom. 9:13)

734. Paul states that, "For whom the Lord loveth," he does what? (Heb. 12:6–7)

735. According to John, if we say that we love God and hate our what, we are a liar? (1 John 4:20)

736. If we love which family members more than Jesus, we are not worthy of Him? (Matt. 10:37)

737. Jesus said that if we love Him, we will keep His what? (John 14:15)

FAMILY AND FELLOW MAN
The Gospel In Action

Solution on page 280

```
H  J  J  X  C  T  H  P  Y  H  I
E  V  I  L  R  N  R  A  S  R  N
K  N  T  L  I  E  P  R  C  S  F
W  C  N  K  R  F  E  E  D  W  I
M  H  B  Q  W  T  J  N  B  R  R
J  I  Y  U  S  I  A  T  Z  F  M
B  L  L  A  N  B  F  S  Y  F  I
L  D  M  Q  S  R  R  E  K  F  T
W  R  M  U  V  N  U  A  L  L  I
R  E  H  F  G  W  E  L  N  M  E
N  N  N  W  L  W  N  W  Y  F  S
```

• According to Paul, servants should be obedient to these. (Eph. 6:5)

• The Colossians were cautioned by Paul not to do this to one another. (Col. 3:9)

  (a) lie
  (b) help
  (c) cheat

• Paul said that this unbelieving partner is sanctified by a believing husband. (1 Cor. 7:12, 14)

• Paul states that children should obey these. (Eph. 6:1)

• Paul said that we that are strong should bear these of the weak. (Rom. 15:1)

  (a) burdens
  (b) infirmities
  (c) debts

• Paul taught that wives are to submit themselves to these partners. (Eph. 5:22)

• Paul admonished Titus not to speak this of any man. (Titus 3:2)

• Paul exhorted the Thessalonians to warn those who were this. (1 Thes. 5:14)

  (a) weak
  (b) unfaithful
  (c) unruly

• Jesus instructed his apostles NOT to forbid these little people to come to Him. (Matt. 19:14)

• Paul exhorted the Thessalonians to support not the strong, but those who are this way. (1 Thes. 5:14)

738. What was the name of the boy who fell asleep during Paul's preaching and fell from a window and died? (Acts 20:9)

739. Quickened by the spirit, where did Jesus go to preach after death? (1 Pet. 3:18–19)

740. The change from death to resurrection is as quick as the what? (1 Cor. 15:52)

741. Death is the "wages" of what? (Rom. 6:23)

742. Paul told the Corinthians that many were sick and slept among them, because they ate the _____ and drank the _____ unworthily. (1 Cor. 11:27–30)

743. What person did Jesus raise from death after he had been in a tomb four days? (John 11:43)

744. What was the foreshadowed method of Peter's death? (2 Pet. 1:14; John 21:18–19)

745. What was the name of the boy Paul raised from the dead? (Acts 20:9–10)

746. How did James, the brother of John, die? (Acts 12:2)

747. Paul declared that in Adam all die, and in what man all are made alive? (1 Cor. 15:22)

748. According to Paul, who had the power of death? (Heb. 2:14)

749. What will all who are in their graves eventually hear and to whom does it belong? (John 5:26–28)

750. Paul said that to live is Christ, and to die is what? (Philip. 1:21)

751. What person acknowledged Jesus as a righteous man when Jesus died on the cross? (Luke 23:47)

752. When Jesus declared oneness with the Father, the Jews took up what, to kill Him? (John 10:31)

753. Who killed James, the brother of John? (Acts 12:1–2)

Trick Question

1306. Paul was in prison when he wrote to Philemon and declared himself to be a what, of Jesus Christ? (Philem. 1:1)

754. Jesus said, "He that hateth me, hateth ___ _____ also." (John 15:23)

755. Judge not according to the appearance, but judge what type judgment? (John 7:24)

756. The Father has committed all judgment unto what person? (John 5:22)

757. Many will come from what directions and sit with Abraham, Isaac, and Jacob in the kingdom of heaven while the "children of the kingdom" are cast out into outer darkness? (Matt. 8:11–12)

758. What did Paul and Barnabus do to condemn the city of Antioch when it rejected them? (Acts 13:51)

759. What was the reason the Lord gave, that we are not to judge? (Matt. 7:1)

760. What did Peter ask, after reminding Jesus that the Apostles had forsaken all to follow Him? (Matt. 19:27)

761. How many need be gathered together for Christ to be in their midst? (Matt. 18:20)

762. After Peter's healing of the lame man and his preaching, how many believed? (Acts 3; 4:4)

763. Paul taught that if we are righteous, our reward is to be joint heirs with whom? (Rom. 8:17)

764. Who knows what we need before we ask? (Matt. 6:8)

765. In the parable of the talents, what was the reward of the second person? (Matt. 25:23)

766. Jesus said that our what, must exceed that of the Scribes and Pharisees, or we cannot enter the kingdom of heaven? (Matt. 5:20)

767. It is life eternal to know whom? (John 17:3)

768. What two "bodies" of the glory of God are mentioned by Paul? (1 Cor. 15:40)

769. In the day of the Lord, we look for new heavens and a new what? (2 Pet. 3:13)

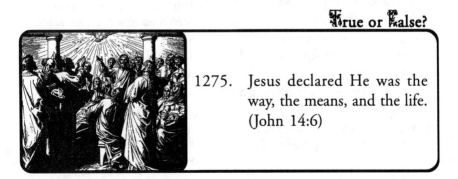

True or False?

1275. Jesus declared He was the way, the means, and the life. (John 14:6)

JUDGMENT AND REWARD
The Gospel In Action

Solution on page 285

Across

3 Peter said the unjust were reserved unto the day of judgment to be _____ . (2 Pet. 2:9)

7 John saw that all of these, both small and great, will stand before God to be judged. (Rev. 20:12)

9 Jesus promised the Apostles that if they endured to the end, they would be this. (Matt. 10:22)

10 The Lord knows how to deliver the godly out of these. (2 Pet. 2:9)

11 Paul taught that if election is by this, then it is no more by works. (Rom. 11:6)

13 All mankind must appear before the judgment seat of this Deity. (2 Cor. 5:10)

17 Although only a few are chosen, many are this. (Matt. 22:14)

19 Paul taught that all will receive their reward according to their what? (1 Cor. 3:8)

21 At the final judgement, we will be required to give account of every idle _____ that we speak. (Matt. 12:36)

24 Because the Apostles had forsaken all and followed Jesus, He promised them these twelve "chairs" as a reward. (Matt. 19:27-28)

25 Jesus used this word to describe the number of mansions in the Father's house. (John 14:2)

26 Paul said that disputations between members are not to be taken to the law, but are to brought before these people. (1 Cor. 6:1)

27 Paul taught that if you take pleasure in unrighteousness, in the judgment you will end up in this state. (2 Thes. 2:12)

Down

1 Paul said he heard unspeakable words when he was caught up into this glorious place. (2 Cor. 12:4)

2 John the Revelator saw this tree in the midst of the paradise of God. (Rev. 2:7)

4 The Lord declared that whosoever would be chief among the Apostles must be this to all. (Matt. 20:27)

5 Paul said, "Render therefore to all their _____ ." (Rom. 13:7)

6 In the Sermon on the Mount, Jesus taught that we will be judged as we do this. (Matt. 7:2)

8 Peter taught that we are given great and precious promises so that we can be partakers of this divine "condition." (2 Pet. 1:4)

12 Jesus declared that it would be more tolerable for Sodom at the judgment day than for this city. (Matt. 11: 23–24)

14 Paul rejoiced because the Corinthians were made sorry after this "holy" manner. (2 Cor. 7:9)

15 Herod was killed by an angel when he did not give glory to this Deity. (Acts 12:23)

16 Paul was taken before this man after Felix, and he sent Paul to be judged by Caesar. (Acts 25:9)

18 James taught that Rahab the harlot was justified by these (synonym for labors). (James 2:25)

20 When the tares are gathered in at the time of harvest, this will be their fate. (Matt. 13:30)

22 Paul declared to the Philippians to forget all things past and press toward this reward. (Philip. 3:14)

23 Paul said that God will render unto every man according to these acts done in the flesh. (Rom. 2:6)

770. In the parable of the wheat and tares, who is the person who sowed the good seed? (Matt. 13:37)

771. How did the rich man eat in the parable of Lazarus and the rich man? (Luke 16:19)

772. In the parable of the hidden treasure, what was the cost of the hidden treasure? (Matt. 13:44)

773. In the parable of the unmerciful servant, how much debt was owed by the fellow servant? (Matt. 18:28)

774. In the parable of the laborers in the vineyard, what wage was promised to all laborers but the first? (Matt. 20:4)

775. In the parable of the two sons, what was the second son's answer and resulting action? (Matt. 21:30)

776. In the parable of the wicked husbandmen, what did the husbandmen do to the first servants that were sent from the householder? (Matt. 21:35)

777. What is the common name of the parable teaching the need to have mercy toward each other? (Matt. 18:23–35)

778. In the parable of the unjust judge, why did the unjust judge say he would grant the widow's petition? (Luke 18:5)

779. In the parable of the talents, who received the third person's talent? (Matt. 25:28)

780. In the parable of the wheat and the tares, what is the meaning of the tares? (Matt. 13:38)

781. In the parable of the ten virgins, what did the foolish virgins ask of the wise virgins? (Matt. 25:8)

782. In the parable of the sower, who "catcheth away" those who receive the seed by the wayside? (Matt. 13:19)

783. In the parable of the two sons, what was the first son's response and resulting action to his father's request? (Matt. 21:29)

784. In the parable of the talents, where was the third person cast for his failure? (Matt. 25:30)

785. What is the common name of the parable that involved the hiring of laborers and their wages? (Matt. 20:1–16)

786. The actions of what parabolic unjust person were commended? (Luke 16:8)

787. The lawyer was trying to justify himself and asked the Lord what question (which produced the parable of the good Samaritan)? (Luke 10:29)

788. In the parable of the king's son, what did the wedding guest NOT have on at the marriage feast? (Matt. 22:11)

789. What parable is similar to the parable of the marriage of the king's son? (Luke 14:16)

PARABLES WORD SEARCH
The Gospel In Action

Solution on page 291

P	L	R	F	R	U	I	T	F	K	J
G	R	T	H	O	R	N	S	P	R	A
P	O	I	C	J	A	B	T	Q	Z	W
V	M	D	S	H	W	U	L	D	W	I
H	N	S	C	O	Q	Y	Y	E	B	D
K	L	R	L	C	N	N	N	V	L	O
V	E	N	G	E	N	X	H	I	C	W
M	A	N	Y	E	P	K	O	L	X	T
M	R	P	P	Y	M	T	H	I	E	F
D	R	O	O	T	Z	T	F	W	Q	Q
S	C	O	R	C	H	E	D	M	V	P

- In the parable of the pearl of great price, this man was seeking goodly pearls. (Matt. 13:45)

  (a) shepherd
  (b) merchant
  (c) priest

- Jesus warned that if the goodman of the house knew in which watch this person was coming, he would have watched. (Matt. 24:43)

  (a) helper
  (b) Levite
  (c) thief

- The judge in the parable of the unjust judge did NOT fear this Deity. (Luke 18:2)

  (a) God
  (b) woman
  (c) widows

- The wise virgins of the parable told the foolish virgins to use this method to get oil for their lamps. (Matt. 25:9)

  (a) steal
  (b) borrow
  (c) buy

- In the parable of the ten virgins, the

wise virgins took this extra, and the unwise did not. (Matt. 25:4)

(a) food
(b) coats
(c) oil

- In the parable of the sower, the fourth seed brought forth this. (Matt. 13:23)

- In the parable of the unmerciful servant, the unmerciful servant put his fellow servant in here. (Matt. 18:30)

(a) jail
(b) his house
(c) prison

- Who was the enemy that sowed the tares in the parable of the wheat and tares? (Matt. 13:39)

- The wage paid to those who labored to the eleventh hour in the parable of the laborers in the vineyard was a how much? (Matt. 20:9)

(a) talent
(b) drachma
(c) penny

- In the parable of the sower, the seeds

that fell on stony places died because they had no what? (Matt. 13:6)

(a) water
(b) nourishment
(c) root

- All the virgins, while waiting for the bridegroom in the parable of the ten virgins, did this. (Matt. 25:5)

- Who was the petitioner in the parable of the unjust judge? (Luke 18:3)

- Who did the judge NOT regard in the parable of the unjust judge? (Luke 18:2)

- The third seed fell among these in the parable of the sower? (Matt. 13:7)

(a) rocks
(b) thorns
(c) weeds

- The sun did this to the second seed in the parable of the sower? (Matt. 13:6)

(a) burned
(b) dried
(c) scorched

Trick Question

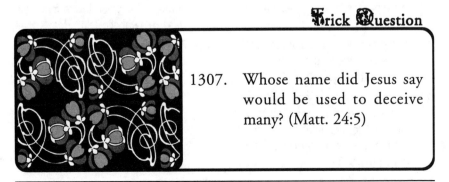

1307. Whose name did Jesus say would be used to deceive many? (Matt. 24:5)

PARABLES CROSSWORD
The Gospel In Action

Solution on page 291

Across

3   In the parable of Lazarus and the rich man, the rich man's clothes are described as being made of what fine material? (Luke 16:19)

6   In the Good Samaritan parable, both a Levite and a member of what other order passed by the injured man without helping him? (Luke 10:31)

9   In the parable of the marriage of the king's son, the king acquired guests from what route? (Matt. 22:10)

11 In parable, the kingdom of heaven is compared to a householder who went out to hire what type of workmen for his vineyard (modern spelling)? (Matt. 20:1)

12 In the parable of Lazarus and the rich man, what did Lazarus eat from the rich man's table? (Luke 16:21)

16 The parable of the unjust what, taught that man should always pray? (Luke 18:2)

17 What was the kingdom of heaven compared to when it was found hidden in a parabolic field? (Matt. 13:44)

22 The first recorded parable in Matthew is the parable of the what? (Matt. 13:3)

24 In the parable of the talents, how many talents were given to the first person? (Matt. 25:15)

25 In parable, what kind of seed was sown amongst the wheat by the enemy? (Matt. 13:25)

27 In the parable of the three measures of meal, the kingdom of heaven is described as what? (Matt. 13:33)

29 In the parable of Lazarus and the rich man, where did the rich man go after he died? (Luke 16:23)

30 In the parable of the talents, the reward of the first servant was to be made this over many things. (Matt. 25:21)

31 When the Bridegroom came, all ten virgins in the parable arose and trimmed their what? (Matt. 25:7)

32 In the parable of the unmerciful servant, if we forgive not our brothers we are delivered to the what? (Matt. 18:34)

Down

1 In the parable of the laborers in the vineyard, the wage that was agreed upon between the first laborers and the householder was a what? (Matt. 20:2)

2 In the parable of the good Samaritan, both a priest and what other official passed by without helping the wounded man? (Luke 10:32)

4 In the parable of the talents, how many talents did the third person gain? (Matt. 25:25-27)

5 This is where the first seed fell in the parable of the sower. (Matt. 13:4)

6 In the parable of the laborers in the vineyard, the laborers that were hired first complained that the others received equal what? (Matt. 20:12)

7 In the parable of the talents, how many talents did the second person gain? (Matt. 25:17)

8 In the parable of the pearl of great price, what was the cost of the pearl? (Matt. 13:46)

10 The only parable that is unique to Mark is commonly known as the seed growing in what covert manner? (Mark 4:26-29)

13 In the parable of the mustard seed, what were lodged in the branches of the grown mustard tree? (Matt. 13:32)

14 In one of the Lord's parables, who was justified after he prayed (it was not the Pharisee)? (Luke 18:13-14)

15 This parable involved a Publican and a man from what religious class? (Luke 18:10)

17 In the parable of the leaven, how many measures of meal did the woman use? (Matt. 13:33)

18 This was the condition of the soil that the second seed fell upon in the parable of the sower. (Matt. 13:5)

19 In the parable of the rich man and Lazarus, this is the color of the clothes the rich man wore. (Luke 16:19)

20 In parable, what was the kingdom of heaven compared to that was cast in the sea? (Matt. 13:47)

21 In the parable of the ten virgins, at what hour did the cry go up that the "Bridegroom cometh"? (Matt. 25:6)

23 In the parable of the wheat and tares, the field represented the what? (Matt. 13:38)

26 The merchant in the parable of the kingdom of heaven was seeking what goodly gems? (Matt. 13:45)

28 In the parable of the ten virgins, the foolish virgin's lamps had gone what? (Matt. 25:8)

Solution on page 299

Across

4   According to John the Revelator, the 144,000 are selected from these tribes. (Rev. 7:4)

5   Those that neither sow, reap, nor gather, yet God feeds them, are these (singular). (Matt. 6:26)

8   Paul taught that after the testator is dead, the testament is in what? (Heb. 9:17)

9   The unique instruction of Jesus to the healed leper, even though He told him to show himself to the priest, was

that he should tell this many about his healing. (Matt. 8:4)

12   Jesus said that before Abraham, was this Deity (a recognized name of Jehovah). (John 8:58)

13   People laid their sick in the streets, hoping that this evidence of Peter's passing might pass over them. (Acts 5:15)

14   This is the name of the individual healed by Jesus as a result of physical violence. (John 18:10)

16   The food of John the Baptist was honey and these. (Matt. 3:4)

19 How many baskets of leftovers were taken up after the feeding of the four thousand? (Matt. 15:37)

22 This word was spoken by Jesus to heal the one deaf and dumb. (Mark 7:34–35)

23 Paul said that there is but this one eternal Being unto us, namely the Father. (1 Cor. 8:6)

25 This is the number of the mark of the beast as recorded in Revelation. (Rev. 13:18)

27 In the miracle contained in John 9, the victim acquire his malady at this time of his life. (John 9:1)

28 In John the Revelator's vision, the beast is wounded with a deadly wound to this physical location on its body. (Rev. 13:3)

30 The death of this King brought Joseph, Mary, and the baby Jesus back from Egypt. (Matt. 2:15)

31 The water pots were available at the Cana marriage because they were normally used for this. (John 2:6)

Down

1 According to John the Revelator, the new name that each who overcomes the world will receive is written on this hard white object. (Rev. 2:17)

2 Paul performed this ordinance a second time on some Ephesian disciples. (Acts 19:5)

3 This is where Jesus was when the prayer recorded in John 17 was uttered.

6 In the parable of the wheat and tares, the harvest represented the end of this. (Matt. 13:39)

7 Jesus healed this man's son from a distance by using only His word. (John 4:46)

10 Paul taught that we should wrestle against spiritual wickedness in these elevated places. (Eph. 6:12)

11 This man was transported by the Spirit after he baptized a eunuch. (Acts 8:39)

15 For using Jesus' name without authority, evil spirits overcame the seven exorcist sons of this person. (Acts 19:13–16)

17 Peter commented in his second epistle that Paul's writings were hard to what? (2 Pet. 3:16)

18 According to John the Revelator, this lasted one-half hour in heaven when the seventh seal in Revelation was opened. (Rev. 8:1)

20 Apparently, Paul wrote to the Corinthians this many times. (2 Cor. 13:1)

21 The title on Christ's cross was written in Hebrew, Greek, and this language. (John 19:20)

23 According to Paul, the ancients were also preached this. (Heb. 4:2)

24 The Sermon on the Mount requires us to "resist not" this. (Matt. 5:39)

26 Philip was transported to another city by this very unique method. (Acts 8:39)

29 1 Corinthians 15:29 speaks of baptism for these who had already passed on.

790. In the parable of the ten virgins, how many virgins are wise? (Matt. 25:2)

791. In the parable of the marriage of the king's son, what was the answer to the first bidding of those who had been invited to the wedding? (Matt. 22:3)

792. In the parable of the sower, where did the fourth group of seeds fall? (Matt. 13:8)

793. What is the parable that is similar to the parable of the talents? (Luke 19:11, 13)

794. In the parable of the sower, what ate the first seed? (Matt. 13:4)

795. In the parable of the sower, what overcame the second seed? (Matt. 13:21)

796. In the parable of the sower, what was the fate of the third seed? (Matt. 13:7)

797. In the parable of the sower, what choked the third seed? (Matt. 13:22)

798. Who was the last parabolic person that was sent to receive the fruits of the wicked husbandmen? (Matt. 21:37)

799. In the parable of the hidden treasure, what did the parabolic man buy so he could acquire the treasure after he found it? (Matt. 13:44)

Let's Get Organized

VI

843. What was the occupation of Matthew? (Matt. 10:3)

844. What was the occupation of Barjesus? (Acts 13:6)

845. What was Luke's profession? (Col. 4:14)

846. What trade had Jesus learned in his early years? (Mark 6:3)

847. Which Apostle was a tentmaker? (Acts 18:1–3)

848. What was the profession of Peter and Andrew? (Matt. 4:18)

849. Peter, James, and John were fisherman when they were called to be Apostles. They followed Jesus and become what? (Matt. 4:19)

True or False?

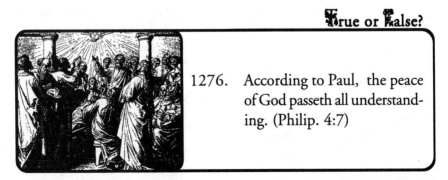

1276. According to Paul, the peace of God passeth all understanding. (Philip. 4:7)

Solution on page 276

Across

1 Paul taught that the Apostles and prophets were this part of a symbolic church. (Eph 2:20)

4 The church organization itself will last until everyone comes to a unity of this (Eph. 4:13)

5 According to Paul, God set these officers first in the church. (1 Cor. 12:28)

9 Paul taught that deacons should not be greedy of this filthy item. (1 Tim. 3:8)

12 Paul commended this woman (a servant of the church at Cenchrea) to the Roman Saints. (Rom. 16:1)

15 John the Revelator stated in his letter to Sardis that the Lord knew a few in Sardis had not defiled these. (Rev. 3:4)

18 Paul states that the symbolic building representing the fitly framed church grows into this holy building. (Eph. 2:21)

20 Paul teaches that these humans should be silent in the church. (1 Cor. 14:34)

21 Paul taught that Bishops should do this well in their own house. (1 Tim. 3:4)

22 Paul ordained these officers in every church. (Acts 14:23)

24 Paul taught that one of the reasons for the church was for the _____ of the Saints. (Eph. 4:12)

Down

2 Paul, addressing the Philippians, mentions the saints, bishops, and this other church officer beginning with the letter "D." (Philip. 1:1)

3 This church office named by Paul begins with the letter "T." (Eph. 4:11)

4 Paul states that apostates will turn away from truth and turn it into this type of story telling. (2 Tim. 4:4)

6 This man made havoc with the early church before he was converted. (Acts 8:3)

7 John the Revelator addresses the book of Revelation to this number of churches by name. (Rev. 1:11)

8 In Philippians, Paul mentions this church office beginning with the letter "B" (singular). (Philip. 1:1)

10 John declares that he will not write a new one of these for the church. (1 John 2:7)

11 This is the church office named by Paul in Ephesians that begins with the letter "E" (singular). (Eph. 4:11)

12 This church office named by Paul begins with the letter "P" (singular). (Eph. 4:11)

13 Paul taught that the Apostles are first in the church, and these are second. (1 Cor. 12:28)

14 Paul said that bishops in reproach fall into the snare of this evil entity. (1 Tim. 3:7)

16 Matthew reports that Jesus told Peter he would build His church upon this hard object. (Matt. 16:18)

17 In Acts, who daily added to the church "such as should be saved"? (Acts 2:47)

19 Paul taught that the church organization is for the work of this. (Eph. 4:12)

23 This came upon the church after they heard of the death of Ananias and Sapphira. (Acts 5:11)

Trick Question

1308. Paul taught that hope that is seen is not what? (Rom. 8:24)

800. Paul instructed Titus that a bishop must be a lover of what? (Titus 1:8)

801. Paul wrote to the bishops, deacons, and the _____ in Philippi. (Philip. 1:1)

802. What was the Galilean's common place of worship called? (Matt. 4:23)

803. How many men did the Apostles call to assist them in the temporal work among the Saints? (Acts 6:3)

804. Who was the first named of the seven assistants called by the Apostles? (Acts 6:5)

805. Did Paul say God had "set forth the Apostles" first or last? (1 Cor. 4:9)

806. Paul describes the office of deacon in his epistle to what person? (1 Tim. 3:8–13)

807. James taught that the elders should do what, when praying over the sick? (James 5:14)

808. Paul stated that one of the reasons for the officers in the church was to do what, for the body of Christ? (Eph. 4:12)

809. What member of the seven, called by the Apostles, preached in Samaria? (Acts 8:5)

810. Paul taught that deacons should be grave, not what? (1 Tim. 3:8)

811. Paul taught that bishops should be of good behavior and apt to what? (1 Tim. 3:2)

812. Paul said that Elders who rule worthily, are worthy of how much honor? (1 Tim. 5:17)

813. Paul taught that a bishop should be experienced, and not a what? (1 Tim. 3:6)

True or False?

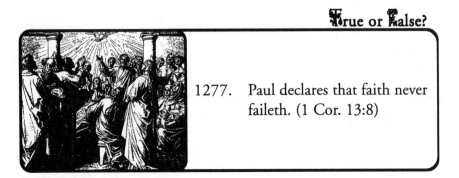

1277. Paul declares that faith never faileth. (1 Cor. 13:8)

814. Scholars generally believe that one of the Apostles had three names. One name was Judas, the other two were _____ and _____. (Matt. 10:3; Mark 3:18; Luke 6:16)

815. Which faithful Apostle was not present when Jesus first appeared to the Apostles in the upper room after the resurrection? (John 20:24)

816. What are the names of the sons of Zebedee who were called to be Apostles? (Matt. 4:21)

817. What member of the Twelve did Jesus call a devil? (John 6:70–71)

818. Which Apostle told Nathanael of Jesus? (John 1:45)

819. In Matthew, what are the names of the first two future Apostles Jesus saw as He walked by the sea of Galilee? (Matt. 4:18)

820. Who became the new Apostle after the death of Judas? (Acts 1:26)

821. What is the name of the Apostle designated as a Canaanite? (Luke 6:15; Mark 3:18)

822. What is the name of the Apostle that is referred to as the son of Alphaeus? (Luke 6:15)

823. What are the two names of the Apostle that is referred to as a publican and the son of Alphaeus? (Matt. 10:3; Mark 2:14)

824. Scholars believe the Apostle Bartholomew had a second name, what was it? (John 1:45; Matthew 10:3)

825. What is the name of the Apostle who wrote Romans? (Rom. 1:1)

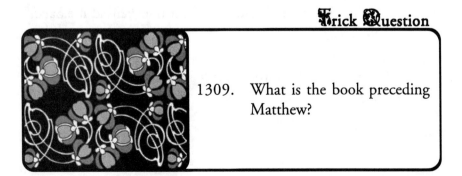

Trick Question

1309. What is the book preceding Matthew?

826. What is the name or appellation of the Apostle that leaned on Jesus' bosom at the Last Supper? (John 13:23)

827. What did Jesus give the Apostles so that they could bind on earth and in heaven? (Matt. 16:19)

828. Paul declared to the Galatians that he was an Apostle, not by man, but by whom? (Gal. 1:1)

829. What did the high priest do to the Apostles (after Jesus' crucifixion) after they had done so many miracles? (Acts 5:18)

830. Which Apostle did Herod arrest because it pleased the Jews? (Acts 12:3–4)

831. Approximately how many were gathered together when the Apostles met before the choosing of Matthias? (Acts 1:15)

832. What was the name of the second Apostle to arrive at the sepulcher? (John 20:4)

833. To which Apostle did Jesus say, "Get thee behind me Satan"? (Matt. 16:23)

834. What is the name of the Apostle that initially refused to have Jesus wash his feet? (John 13:8)

835. Who did Paul consider the Apostle and High Priest of his profession? (Heb. 3:1)

836. What did the disciples do when Jesus entered the boat after walking on the water? (Matt. 14:33)

837. What was the name of the Apostle that will tarry on earth until Jesus comes again? (John 21:22–23)

838. Jesus said that by doing what to the Apostles, some would think that they did God service? (John 16:2)

839. Which Apostle was a Canaanite? (Matt. 10:4)

840. What was the Apostles' reaction when the saw Jesus with the Samaritan woman by the well? (John 4:27)

841. On their first mission, the Lord instructed the Apostles to only go to whom? (Matt. 10:6)

842. Who said he was not a whit behind the chiefest Apostles? (2 Cor. 11:5)

Solution on page 274

R	M	L	V	V	X	S	G	T	C	R	M	S
M	T	K	J	T	T	I	R	R	G	L	E	A
K	G	W	N	E	F	G	Q	N	W	T	F	M
H	E	K	N	H	A	T	E	D	I	P	R	A
L	N	C	P	N	J	G	C	N	R	H	I	R
N	T	J	T	V	N	T	A	Y	Z	R	E	I
Z	I	O	E	L	S	A	G	G	V	Q	N	T
P	L	K	K	S	N	A	C	X	P	K	D	A
Q	E	P	L	A	U	B	U	C	Y	N	S	N
Z	S	T	C	G	L	S	T	L	W	L	K	S
B	R	Y	E	D	I	D	Y	M	U	S	M	W
R	R	W	G	R	M	N	N	X	P	A	U	L
M	I	N	I	S	T	E	R	H	Y	L	K	Y

- Matthew states that James and John were mending these when Jesus called them to follow Him. (Matt. 4:21)

- Jesus said the Apostles would be this of all men for His name's sake. (Matt. 10:22)
  - (a) hated
  - (b) shunned
  - (c) loved

- Paul said he withstood this Apostle to his face at Antioch because he was to be blamed. (Gal 2:11)
  - (a) John
  - (b) James
  - (c) Peter

- At the Last Supper the Apostles were no longer called servants by Jesus, but this. (John 15:15)

- The second Simon of the Twelve Apostles was also called this to distinguish him from Peter. (Matt. 10:4)
  - (a) Judean
  - (b) Roman
  - (c) Canaanite

- This Apostle was called Mercurius by the people of Lystra. (Acts 14:12)

- This person was called to be an Apostle at the same time as Barnabus. (Acts 13:2)

- Paul declared himself to be the Apostle sent to this group of people. (Rom. 11:13)

- Jesus said He first saw Nathanael sitting under this kind of tree. (John 1:49–50)

- To be great among his brethren, an Apostle had to become this to all. (Matt. 20:26)
  (a) minister
  (b) servant
  (c) helper

- The name of the person who chose the Apostles. (John 15:16)

- When Jesus first sent the Apostles on their missions, He commanded them not to enter any cities of this civilization. (Matt. 10:5)

- The method the eleven Apostles used to select the new Apostle to replace Judas was by this means (singular). (Acts 1:26)

- The Apostle Thomas was also called by this name. (John 11:16)

True or False?

1278. John said that Jesus' "brethren" did not believe in Him. (John 7:5)

850. What gift of the Spirit was manifested to the multitude at Pentecost? (Acts 2:6)

851. What was the topic of Peter's discourse on the day of Pentecost? (Acts 2:24)

852. Peter taught on Pentecost that the sepulcher of what king of Israel was still with them at that time? (Acts 2:29)

853. What sound did the Apostles hear in heaven on the day of Pentecost? (Acts 2:2)

854. Which of the Apostles healed the lame man after Pentecost? (Acts 3:2, 6)

855. What were the Apostles accused of being as they preached to the crowd on the day of Pentecost? (Acts 2:13)

856. What was the gift of the Spirit manifest by the Apostles at Pentecost? (Acts 2:4)

857. What is the first recorded healing by the Apostles after Pentecost? (Acts 3:2, 7)

858. What Old Testament prophet was quoted on Pentecost as having his prophesy fulfilled? (Acts 2:16–17)

859. What sat upon each of the Apostles at Pentecost? (Acts 2:3)

860. What did the church members have in common after Pentecost? (Acts 2:44)

861. In the mouth of two or three what, shall every word be established? (2 Cor. 13:1)

862. Paul stated that Apollos had watered and God had given the increase. What had Paul done? (1 Cor. 3:6)

863. Who decided whether converted Gentiles must live the Law of Moses or not? (Acts 15:13, 19)

864. According to James, the sick should call for whom? (James 5:14)

865. When did Paul say he had been called to serve? (2 Tim. 1:9)

866. Jesus told Nicodemus that a man must be born of what two things if he is to enter the Kingdom of God? (John 3:5)

867. What did the Apostles use to anoint with when healing and blessing the sick? (Mark 6:13)

868. What does James say brings confusion and every evil work? (James 3:16)

869. Jesus said that if you humble yourself, you will be what? (Matt. 23:12)

870. Paul taught that bishops should not be greedy of what? (1 Tim. 3:3)

871. We should be what, and not hearers of the word only? (James 1:22)

BODY PARTS WORD SEARCH

Let's Get Organized

Solution on page 275

```
P  F  L  P  N  N  Q  H  E  A  R  T  D  T  R
R  K  Q  T  Z  L  Y  C  C  Q  I  E  X  C  M
C  R  T  G  C  Z  N  B  X  E  L  K  A  H  X
E  O  R  N  L  N  K  Z  C  I  D  N  F  I  L
N  K  M  N  A  B  M  E  F  K  L  M  R  L  N
E  D  W  M  Y  V  D  E  S  N  G  G  A  D  M
M  G  S  O  U  L  D  P  O  P  D  Q  I  R  T
I  V  X  V  C  N  K  S  E  T  I  L  D  E  R
E  Z  E  A  R  S  I  V  Q  A  C  R  L  N  T
S  M  L  T  T  O  E  C  F  M  C  N  I  F  C
M  W  R  H  P  U  X  G  A  L  P  E  C  T  M
N  R  L  K  G  L  M  B  I  T  E  N  W  K  J
F  P  R  N  W  H  X  V  K  P  I  S  T  H  L
Y  V  O  K  S  T  E  P  H  E  N  O  H  M  G
N  T  U  N  B  E  L  I  E  F  M  Q  N  X  N
```

- James said no man can tame the tongue because it is unruly and full of this deadly thing. (James 3:8)

- Jesus said to fear not them who can kill the body, but cannot kill this. (Matt. 10:28)

- James said that the body without this is dead. (James 2:26)

- Paul taught that our spirit bears witness that we are this of God. (Rom. 8:16)

  (a) offspring
  (b) children
  (c) begotten

- In the Sermon on the Mount, Jesus declared that the whole body was dark if the eye is full of this. (Matt. 6:23)

- Paul said apostates shall turn away these appendages on the head from truth unto fables. (2 Tim. 4:4)

- John stated that the Word was made this. (John 1:14)

  (a) spirit
  (b) body
  (c) flesh

- Jesus said, "Let not your heart be troubled, neither let it be _____." (John 14:27)

- Jesus said that to eat with unwashed hands does not do this to a man. (Matt. 15:20)

  (a) defile
  (b) hurt
  (c) condemn

- This is one of the seven called by the Apostles. He saw God, and Jesus on his right, hand before he was stoned. (Acts 7:55, 59)

- Paul said that to be spiritually minded is life and this. (Rom. 8:6)

  (a) glory
  (b) goodness
  (c) peace

- Jesus anointed the eyes of the one born blind with this substance after spitting upon the ground. (John 9:6)

- Paul declared that none of this should proceed out of our mouths if it is corrupt. (Eph. 4:29)

  (a) words
  (b) communication
  (c) shouting

- James taught that we both bless God and curse men with this little "member." (James 3:8–9)

- Eye hath not seen nor ear heard that which has entered into this part of man. (1 Cor. 2:9)

  (a) mind
  (b) thoughts
  (c) heart

- Paul said that Jesus must reign until He has put all of these under His feet. (1 Cor. 15:25)

- Paul cautioned his brethren not to have an evil heart of this. (Heb. 3:12)

  (a) sorrow
  (b) unbelief
  (c) distress

- Paul said that with their tongues, the unrighteous have used this. (Rom. 3:13)

  (a) lie
  (b) falsehood
  (c) deceit

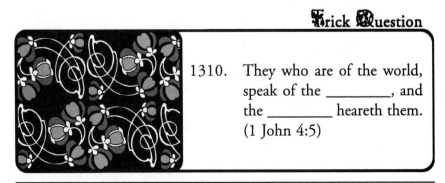

Trick Question

1310. They who are of the world, speak of the _____, and the _____ heareth them. (1 John 4:5)

872. Paul said that the priesthood was changed; therefore, it also required a change in what? (Heb. 7:12)

873. Paul said that Moses spake nothing concerning the priesthood of what tribe? (Heb. 7:14)

874. Paul declared that no man takes honor to himself, "but he that is called of God, as was" who? (Heb. 5:4)

875. Paul said if perfection came by what priesthood, there is no need for the order of Melchizedek? (Heb. 7:11)

876. Paul declared that Jesus was a priest forever after the order of whom? (Heb. 5:6)

877. According to Peter, we are a royal priesthood and what type of people? (1 Pet. 2:9)

878. What is the name of the angel that appeared to Zacharias and told him of the forthcoming birth of John? (Luke 1:19)

879. What will the angels sound at Christ's coming? (Matt. 24:31)

880. How did the angel appear to Joseph, the espoused of Mary? (Matt. 1:20)

881. What archangel contended and disputed with the devil over the body of Moses? (Jude 1:9)

882. When the angel appeared at Jesus' tomb, the soldiers guarding the tomb became as what? (Matt. 28:4)

883. Paul states that if you entertain what people, you may be entertaining angels unawares? (Heb. 13:2)

884. How many people of the earth are to be killed by the four angels that will be loosed by the sixth angel with a trumpet? (Rev. 9:15)

885. The angel told Mary that Jesus would save the people from their what? (Matt. 1:21)

886. When Mary Magdalene saw the angel at Jesus's sepulcher, his countenance was described as being like what? (Matt. 28:3)

887. According to Paul, what evil entity was transformed into an angel of light? (2 Cor. 11:14)

888. What did the angel declare to the women at Christ's sepulcher when they saw that it was empty? (Matt. 28:6)

889. John the Revelator said that he saw another angel who flew through the heavens, having the everlasting what? (Rev. 14:6)

890. God cast the angels that sinned down to where? (2 Pet. 2:4)

891. In John the Revelator's vision, how many men were "sealed" by an angel up to salvation? (Rev. 7:4)

892. Jude said the angels who kept not which estate, are in everlasting chains? (Jude 1:6)

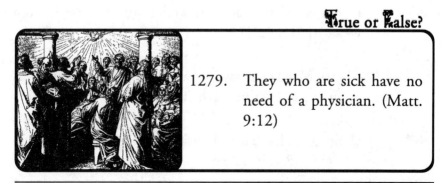

True or False?

1279. They who are sick have no need of a physician. (Matt. 9:12)

893. How long did Felix leave Paul bound to please the Jews? (Acts 24:27)

894. Paul was sent as a prisoner from Jerusalem to what governor? (Acts 23:24)

895. What caused all the prison doors to open when Paul was in prison? (Acts 16:26)

896. Whose house did Peter go to after an angel released him from Herod's prison? (Acts 12:12)

897. What was the length of time Paul spent in Rome during his first imprisonment? (Acts 28:30)

898. Who opened the prison doors to allow the Apostles to leave? (Acts 5:19)

899. Who released Peter from Herod's prison? (Acts 12:7)

900. What person should you agree with quickly, or you might be cast into prison? (Matt. 5:25)

901. Where did Paul stay while a prisoner in Rome? (Acts 28:30)

902. Paul converted what person because of a miracle that was performed while he was in prison? (Acts 16:27, 33)

903. Who stood by Paul in prison at night after his arrest in Jerusalem? (Acts 23:11)

904. Paul declared to the Ephesians that he was a prisoner for whom? (Eph. 3:1)

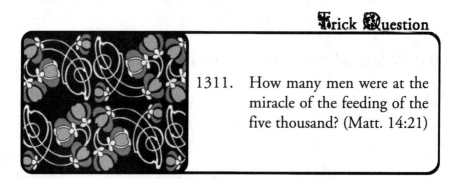

1311. How many men were at the miracle of the feeding of the five thousand? (Matt. 14:21)

905. Peter said that he would always stir us up by putting us in what of his teachings? (2 Pet. 1:13)

    a. repentance
    b. remembrance
    c. understanding

906. At which watch of the night did Jesus walk upon the water? (Matt. 14:25)

    a. first
    b. third
    c. fourth

907. How many chapters are in 1Timothy?

    a. five
    b. seven
    c. six

908. What did the Jews believe troubled the water at the pool of Bethesda? (John 5:4)

    a. an angel
    b. a spirit
    c. a ghost

909. What was the amount of talents owed by the parabolic unmerciful servant? (Matt. 18:24)

    a.   5,000
    b.   15,000
    c.   10,000

910. Jesus told the Samaritan woman by the well that she had already had how many husbands? (John 4:18)

    a.   three
    b.   five
    c.   two

911. What we should NOT sound when giving our alms? (Matt. 6:2)

    a.   a shout
    b.   a horn
    c.   a trumpet

912. What did the foolish virgins in the parable fail to take with them? (Matt. 25:3–4)

    a.   lamps
    b.   oil
    c.   extra oil

913. What was the reason Peter ceased to walk on the water? (Matt. 14:30)

    a.   doubt
    b.   fear
    c.   shame

914. What is the total number of generations from Abraham to Christ? (Matt. 1:17)

    a.   14
    b.   28
    c.   42

915. The first instruction to Peter on the Galilean shore after the resurrection was to feed the Lord's what? (John 21:15)

    a.   sheep
    b.   lambs
    c.   ewes

916. Paul stated that the laborer is worthy of his what? (1 Tim. 5:18)

    a.   hire
    b.   reward
    c.   wages

917. Where were the members of Christ's church first called Christians? (Acts 11:26)

    a.   Athens
    b.   Corinth
    c.   Antioch

918. In the parable of the talents, how many talents were given the second person? (Matt. 25:15)

    a.   2
    b.   5
    c.   10

919. Jesus is our what, with the Father? (1 John 2:1)

    a.   petitioner
    b.   advocate
    c.   helper

920. In the Lord's prayer, we ask God to forgive our what? (Matt. 6:12)

    a.   sins
    b.   debts
    c.   enemies

921. How many loaves were available at the feeding of the four thousand? (Matt. 15:34)

    a.   seven
    b.   five
    c.   three

922. According to Paul, how are things of God discerned? (1 Cor. 2:14)

    a.   temporally
    b.   spiritually
    c.   naturally

923. Speaking of Paul's writings, Peter states that they are hard to what? (2 Pet. 3:15–16)

    a.   understand
    b.   comprehend
    c.   fathom

924. How many times had Paul prayed to have the thorn in his flesh removed? (2 Cor. 12:8)

    a.   1
    b.   3
    c.   5

925. When Paul and Barnabus split because of the contention between them, Barnabus took which companion with him? (Acts 15:39)

    a.   Timothy
    b.   John Mark
    c.   Luke

926. How many times did Paul say he had been stoned? (2 Cor. 11:25)

    a.   once
    b.   twice
    c.   three times

927. How long will the two witnesses in Revelation prophesy? (Rev. 11:3)

    a.   42 months
    b.   1260 days
    c.   3 and one half years

Search The Scriptures

VII

928. What is the full name of the book of Acts?

929. What are the names of the three Synoptics or Synoptic Gospels?

930. What is the full name of Colossians?

931. What is the full name of 2 Corinthians?

932. What is the full name of the book of Ephesians?

933. What is the last word of the Book of Revelation?

934. How many Epistles did Paul write to the Galatians?

935. What is the full name of 1 Thessalonians?

936. How many Epistles did Paul write to Philemon?

937. What is the full name of 2 John?

938. How many chapters are in 3 John?

939. What distinction is given the verse found in John 11:35?

940. How many chapters are in Jude?

941. What is the full name of the book of Revelation?

942. Which chapter and verse in Philippians contains the "whatsoever things are" recitation by Paul which lists the righteous attributes we should seek?

943. What are the words of the shortest verse in the New Testament? (John 11:35)

944. What is the full name of the book of James?

945. What is the full name of the book of Romans?

946. What is the full name of the New Testament?

947. How many chapters are in Acts?

True or False?

1280. Paul said that if you are spiritual, you should assist one overtaken in a sin. (Gal. 6:1)

1036. Jesus commanded us to be _____, even as our Father in Heaven is _____. (Matt. 5:48)

1037. The healed impotent man who was at the pool of Bethesda was warned by Jesus to sin no more lest a _____ thing might come upon him. (John 5:14)

1038. John states that the "beginning of miracles" by Jesus was when He turned the _____ to _____. (John 2:9, 11)

1039. Paul says that Jesus was the _____ of every creature. (Col. 1:15)

1040. With God, there is no _____ of persons. (Rom. 2:11)

1041. The Lord's raiment looked as white as the _____ at the Transfiguration. (Matt. 17:2)

1042. "What God hath joined together, let no man put _____." (Matt. 19:6)

1043. Herod requested the wise men to return and tell him where the child was, because he said he wanted to _____ him also. (Matt. 2:8)

1044. "_____ is mine; I will _____, saith the Lord." (Rom. 12:19)

1045. To the Corinthians, Paul states that there are _____ many and _____ many. (1 Cor. 8:5)

1046. Simon was declared to be in the _____ of bitterness and the bond of _____ for offering to buy the power of the Apostles. (Acts 8:23)

1047. Paul declared that the _____ killeth, but the _____ giveth life. (2 Cor. 3:6)

1048. Jesus, the bread of life, said come and believe and you will never _____ or _____. (John 6:35)

1049. The Apostles were given the power to both bind and _____ on earth and in heaven. (Matt. 18:18)

1050. Paul declared to Timothy that there was laid up for him in heaven a _____ of righteousness. (2 Tim. 4:8)

1051. False prophets cannot gather grapes and figs from _____ and _____. (Matt. 7:16)

1052. Jesus said that the blind guides of the Jews, strain at a _____ and swallow a _____. (Matt. 23:24)

1053. When pearls are cast before swine, they _____ them under their feet. (Matt. 7:6)

1054. Paul said that in Christ Jesus, neither _____ nor _____ availeth anything. (Gal. 6:15)

1055. "Having a form of godliness, but _____ the power thereof." (2 Tim. 3:5)

1056. Paul states: "Rejoice in the Lord alway: and again I say, _____." (Philip. 4:4)

1057. Paul could do all things through Christ which _____ him. (Philip. 4:13)

1058. The Lord declared that the Apostle's _____ was willing, but their _____ was weak. (Matt. 26:41)

1059. Jesus accused the Jews for teaching as doctrine the _____ of men. (Matt. 15:9)

1060. "The Sabbath was made for _____, and not _____ for the Sabbath." (Mark 2:27)

1061. Paul said that the faith of the _____ was spoken of throughout the world. (Rom. 1:8)

1062. "For our God is a consuming _____." (Heb. 12:29)

1063. Paul, writing to Timothy, calls him his own _____. (1 Tim. 1:2)

1064. John, in introducing his first epistle, testifies that he has both seen and handled the _____ of life. (1 John 1:1)

1065. Paul said to Timothy, "I have fought a _____ _____." (2 Tim. 4:7)

1066. Paul, writing to the Thessalonians, said he remembered their work of _____, their labor of _____, and their patience of _____. (1 Thes. 1:3)

1067. Thomas saw the Lord and believed. Jesus said that blessed are those who have not _____ and yet have believed. (John 20:29)

1068. In Christ, old things have passed away and all has become _____. (2 Cor. 5:17)

1069. Paul said, "I have fought a good fight, I have _____ ___ _____, I have kept the faith." (2 Tim. 4:7)

1070. "Prove all things; hold fast that which is _____." (1 Thes. 5:21)

1071. The Lord prophesied that before His Second Coming, we will hear of _____ and rumors of _____. (Matt. 24:6)

1072. Concerning the tongue: "Behold, how great a matter a little fire _____." (James 3:5)

1073. The nobleman that asked Jesus to heal his son was told that, "Except ye see _____ and _____, ye will not believe." (John 4:48)

1074. Many are called, but _____ are chosen. (Matt. 20:16)

1075. Paul declared that faith was the _____ of things hoped for and the _____ of things not seen. (Heb. 11:1)

1076. Jesus said His yoke was _____ and His burden _____. (Matt. 11:30)

1077. To heal one deaf person, Jesus put His fingers in his _____, and spit and touched his _____. (Mark 7:33)

1078. "O grave, where is thy _____." (1 Cor. 15:55)

1079. Jesus said to render unto Caesar the _____, that are Caesar's and unto God the _____ that are God's. (Matt. 22:21)

1080. Jesus asked if the baptism of John was from _____ or of _____. (Matt. 21:25)

1081. Paul cautioned the Colossians not to be spoiled by _____ and vein _____. (Col. 2:8)

1082. Man was not made for the _____, but the _____ for man. (Mark 2:27)

1083. The phrase, _____ and gnashing of teeth, usually describes what occurs in outer darkness. (Matt. 8:12)

Trick Question

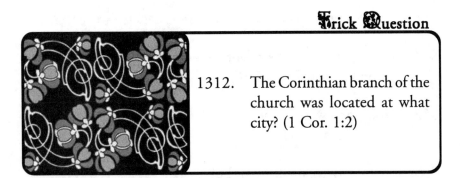

1312. The Corinthian branch of the church was located at what city? (1 Cor. 1:2)

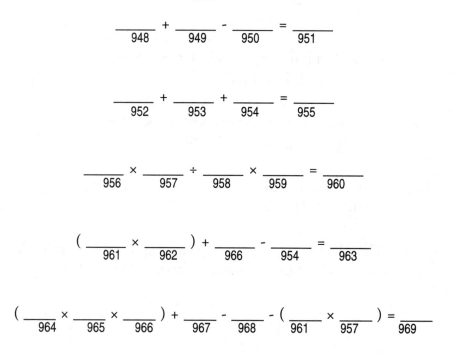

$$\frac{}{948} + \frac{}{949} - \frac{}{950} = \frac{}{951}$$

$$\frac{}{952} + \frac{}{953} + \frac{}{954} = \frac{}{955}$$

$$\frac{}{956} \times \frac{}{957} \div \frac{}{958} \times \frac{}{959} = \frac{}{960}$$

$$(\frac{}{961} \times \frac{}{962}) + \frac{}{966} - \frac{}{954} = \frac{}{963}$$

$$(\frac{}{964} \times \frac{}{965} \times \frac{}{966}) + \frac{}{967} - \frac{}{968} - (\frac{}{961} \times \frac{}{957}) = \frac{}{969}$$

948. How many chapters are in 1 Thessalonians?

949. How many foolish virgins are in the parable of the ten virgins? (Matt. 25:2)

950. How many chapters are in 1 Peter?

951. In the parable of the talents, how many talents did the first person gain? (Matt. 25:16)

952. How many were in the second large group Jesus sent on missions? (Luke 10:1)

953. How many chapters are in Luke?

954. How many chapters are in James?

955. In the parable of the lost sheep, how many of the sheep were left behind? (Matt. 18:12)

956. How many of Paul's Epistles are to individuals?

957. How many chapters are in Philippians?

958. How many days had Lazarus been in the grave when Jesus arrived at Bethany? (John 11:17)

959. How many carried the one sick of the palsy to Jesus to be healed? (Mark 2:3)

960. How many chapters are in 1 Corinthians?

961. How many Epistles did John write?

962. How many Epistles did Paul write?

963. The number that vowed neither to eat nor drink until they killed Paul was over what? (Acts 23:13)

964. How many chapters are in Colossians?

965. How many chapters are in Galatians?

966. How many chapters are in the Gospel of John?

967. In the parable of the laborers in the vineyard, what was the last hour the laborers were hired? (Matt. 20:6)

968. How many chapters are in Titus?

969. According to Paul, Jesus, after the resurrection, was seen of above what large number at once? (1 Cor. 15:6)

*Mathematical operations should be accomplished in the order shown. Thus, 1 + 2 ÷ 3 = 1.
Do not evaluate rows or columns that contain a blacked-out square.*

	+		÷		=	
970		971		972		973
÷		+		=		+
	974		975		976	
=			−		−	
977		978		979		980
+	■	−	■			+
					981	
	−		−		=	
982		983		984		985
=	■	=	■			=
					986	
	−		×		=	
987		988		989		990

970. How many chapters are in Mark?

971. How many chapters are in 1 John?

972. How many chapters are in 2 Peter?

973. In John's vision, how many angels had the seven last plagues? (Rev. 15:1)

974. How many chapters are in Hebrews?

975. How many chapters are in 2 Thessalonians?

976. How many chapters are in Romans?

977. How many chapters are in 2 John?

978. How many chapters are in 2 Corinthians?

979. How many Dieties were seen or heard on the Mount of Transfiguration? (Matt. 17:1, 5)

980. In the parable of the pounds, what was the total number who received the pounds? (Luke 19:13)

981. How many chapters are in 2 Timothy?

982. How many were called by Jesus to be His Apostles? (Matt. 10:2–5)

983. How many souls were saved in the Ark? (1 Pet. 3:20)

984. How many apostles were with Jesus on the Mount of Transfiguration? (Matt. 17:1)

985. How many chapters are in 3 John?

986. James addresses his general epistle to how many of the tribes of Israel? (James 1:1)

987. How many chapters are in Matthew?

988. What was the largest number of lepers healed at one time? (Luke 17:12)

989. In the parable of the talents, how many talents were given to the third person? (Matt. 25:15)

990. How many years the woman had had the spirit of infirmity before she was healed? (Luke 13:11)

True or False?

1281. Jesus said that the poor are always with us. (John 12:8)

KNOW YOUR BOOKS

Search The Scriptures

Solution on page 286

```
B  R  T  W  O  T  H  E  S  S  A  L  O  N  I  A  N  S  L  S  K
T  W  O  P  E  T  E  R  P  J  N  P  N  X  Y  R  J  T  N  H  G
X  V  N  N  O  R  G  B  J  K  A  O  N  H  H  W  Y  A  N  S  P
P  H  N  Y  N  M  R  K  K  N  M  M  T  K  S  E  I  T  N  F  N
K  Q  M  G  E  N  B  P  L  E  R  O  E  N  T  H  B  A  H  F  C
Y  D  A  C  T  S  F  M  L  C  M  N  A  S  T  P  I  R  K  L  O
N  Y  N  T  H  T  J  I  J  I  J  I  K  N  C  H  F  H  E  T  L
K  T  R  E  E  F  H  M  T  Z  T  R  I  J  T  I  L  O  C  W  O
R  H  F  P  S  P  P  O  N  A  N  R  Q  N  D  L  L  N  F  T  S
C  R  R  H  S  C  W  M  L  N  O  V  I  J  L  I  Z  E  Q  L  S
M  E  J  E  A  T  M  A  D  C  N  R  P  Z  K  P  K  P  J  B  I
T  E  B  S  L  Y  G  M  O  M  O  V  J  Y  G  P  K  E  N  N  A
M  J  L  I  O  F  Z  W  M  C  V  D  H  O  T  I  T  T  F  G  N
R  O  M  A  N  S  T  Z  E  A  K  G  O  N  H  A  V  E  W  K  S
R  H  H  N  I  V  L  N  P  Z  T  M  N  N  T  N  W  R  R  Z  J
R  N  M  S  A  T  O  F  G  Y  Q  T  G  T  E  S  T  A  N  Z  X
L  M  M  H  N  D  M  T  W  O  J  O  H  N  I  J  M  K  B  M  T
P  F  N  M  S  M  P  M  D  R  Y  J  G  E  C  T  O  N  J  T  T
C  N  Z  B  T  R  J  G  K  C  B  U  M  H  W  R  U  H  C  L  M
R  K  L  U  K  E  D  L  D  M  X  D  V  G  C  L  H  S  N  G  Z
X  J  G  R  M  G  P  F  Q  O  N  E  T  I  M  O  T  H  Y  N  R
```

- What book precedes Ephesians?

  (a) Philippians
  (b) Galatians
  (c) Colossians

- What book precedes John?

  (a) Matthew
  (b) Luke
  (c) Mark

- What book precedes Philemon?

  (a) Titus
  (b) Two Timothy
  (c) Galatians

- What book precedes Colossians?

  (a) Philippians
  (b) Romans
  (c) Galatians

- What book precedes Hebrews?

  (a) Titus
  (b) James
  (c) Philemon

- What book precedes Romans?

  (a) Acts
  (b) Titus
  (c) Luke

Challenged by the New Testament

- What book precedes Mark?
  - (a) John
  - (b) Luke
  - (c) Matthew
- What book precedes Two Thessalonians?
  - (a) One Thessalonians
  - (b) Colossians
  - (c) Galatians
- What book precedes Luke?
  - (a) John
  - (b) Mark
  - (c) Matthew
- What book precedes One Corinthians?
  - (a) Romans
  - (b) Acts
  - (c) John
- What book precedes One Peter?
  - (a) Hebrews
  - (b) James
  - (c) One Timothy
- What book precedes Two Peter?
  - (a) One Peter
  - (b) James
  - (c) John
- What book precedes Titus?
  - (a) Philemon
  - (b) James
  - (c) Two Timothy
- What book precedes One John?
  - (a) James
  - (b) Two Peter
  - (c) Two John
- What book precedes James?
  - (a) Philemon
  - (b) Hebrews
  - (c) Jude
- What book precedes Revelation?
  - (a) Jude
  - (b) Three John
  - (c) James
- What book precedes Two Corinthians?
  - (a) One Corinthians
  - (b) John
  - (c) Romans
- What book precedes Two Timothy?
  - (a) One Timothy
  - (b) Philemon
  - (c) Two Thessalonians
- What book precedes Galatians?
  - (a) Ephesians
  - (b) Romans
  - (c) Two Corinthians
- What book precedes Two John?
  - (a) James
  - (b) Jude
  - (c) One John
- What book precedes Philippians?
  - (a) James
  - (b) Ephesians
  - (c) Hebrews
- What book precedes Three John?
  - (a) Two John
  - (b) Jude
  - (c) Titus
- What book precedes One Thessalonians?
  - (a) Timothy
  - (b) Colossians
  - (c) Philemon
- What book precedes Acts?
  - (a) Matthew
  - (b) Mark
  - (c) John
- What book precedes Jude?
  - (a) One John
  - (b) Three John
  - (c) Titus
- What book precedes One Timothy?
  - (a) Two Thessalonians
  - (b) Titus
  - (c) Colossians

Solution on page 287

Across

1 What book follows Galatians?

   (a) Ephesians
   (b) Romans
   (c) Philippians

3 What book follows Jude?

   (a) One John
   (b) James
   (c) Revelation

9 What book follows One Thessalonians?

   (a) Timothy
   (b) Titus
   (c) Two Thessalonians

12 What book follows Titus?

   (a) Colossians
   (b) Philemon
   (c) Timothy

14 What book follows Matthew?

   (a) Mark
   (b) Luke
   (c) John

15 What book follows Romans?

   (a) Acts
   (b) Galatians
   (c) One Corinthians

17 What book follows James?

(a) Hebrews
(b) Titus
(c) One Peter

20 What book follows Two Thessalonians?

(a) James
(b) One Timothy
(c) Galatians

21 What book follows Two Peter?

(a) Jude
(b) James
(c) One John

23 What book follows Philippians?

(a) Galatians
(b) Timothy
(c) Colossians

24 What book follows Two John?

(a) Three John
(b) Jude
(c) Revelation

25 What book follows Philemon?

(a) James
(b) Hebrews
(c) Titus

26 What book follows Acts?

(a) James
(b) Romans
(c) One Corinthians

Down

2 What book follows Ephesians?

(a) Galatians
(b) Mark
(c) Philippians

4 What book follows Two Timothy?

(a) Titus
(b) One John
(c) Hebrews

5 What book follows Mark?

(a) John
(b) James
(c) Luke

6 What book follows Hebrews?

(a) Timothy
(b) James
(c) John

7 What book follows One John?

(a) Two John
(b) James
(c) Hebrews

8 What book follows Two Corinthians?

(a) Galations
(b) Acts
(c) Romans

10 What book follows One Corinthians?

(a) Romans
(b) Acts
(c) Two Corinthians

11 What book follows Colossians?

(a) Philipians
(b) OneThessalonians
(c) Romans

13 What book follows One Peter?

(a) James
(b) One John
(c) Two Peter

16 What book follows One Timothy?

(a) Titus
(b) Two Timothy
(c) Hebrews

18 What book follows Luke?

(a) Matthew
(b) Romans
(c) John

19 What book follows John?

(a) Romans
(b) Acts
(c) James

22 What book follows Three John?

(a) James
(b) Jude
(c) Revelation

991. What was the name of Herodias' legal husband? (Matt. 14:3)

992. What is the name of the city where Jesus spent His childhood? (Matt. 2:23)

993. What is the beggar's name in the parable of the rich man? (Luke 16:20)

994. What item is found in Matthew 6:9–13 (common name)?

995. What city did the centurion live in who requested a healing for his servant? (Matt. 8:5)

996. How many generations were there from the Babylonian captivity to Christ? (Matt. 1:17)

997. The Jews believed that the first person in what pool, after the waters were troubled, would be healed? (John 5:2, 4)

998. Jesus indicated that Nicodemus was a what, in Israel? (John 3:10)

999. What was the quantity of the spikenard with which Mary anointed Jesus? (John 12:3)

1000. What type of sepulcher was Lazarus buried in? (John 11:38)

1001. In the parable of Lazarus and the rich man, what was between Lazarus and the rich man after they died? (Luke 16:26)

1002. What is the full name of the book of Matthew?

1003. What did Peter leave behind in order to follow Jesus? (Matt. 4:20)

1004. Jesus was not sent to the call the righteous to repent, but whom? (Matt. 9:13)

1005. Matthew begins his gospel by stating that he is declaring the what, of Jesus? (Matt. 1:1)

1006. What is the shortest Gospel?

Trick Question

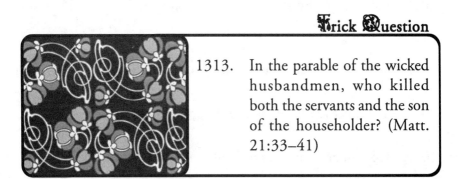

1313. In the parable of the wicked husbandmen, who killed both the servants and the son of the householder? (Matt. 21:33–41)

1007. What is the full name of 2 Timothy?

1008. What is the full name of 1 Corinthians?

1009. How many Epistles did Peter write?

1010. How many Epistles did Paul write to Titus?

1011. Colossians was written from what place?

1012. Philippians was written from what city?

1013. Where was The Epistle of Paul to Philemon written from?

1014. Which two companions were with Paul when he wrote 2 Thessalonians? (2 Thes. 1:1)

1015. Who was Paul's companion when he wrote to the Colossians? (Col. 1:1)

1016. How many Epistles that Paul wrote to the Corinthians are contained in the Bible?

1017. What is the full name of the book of Jude?

1018. What is the full name of Philippians?

1019. How many Epistles did Paul write to the Romans?

1020. 2 Timothy was written from what city?

1021. To whom did John address his second Epistle? (2 John 1:1)

1022. What is the full name of 3 John?

1023. Galatians was written from what city?

1024. What is the full name of 2 Thessalonians?

1025. What is the full name of the book of Philemon?

1026. What is the full name of the book of Titus?

1027. What is the full name of 1 Timothy?

1028. What is the full name of Hebrews?

1029. How many Epistles did Paul write to the Colossians?

1030. What is the full name of 2 Peter?

1031. To what churches was the Epistle to the Galatians written? (Gal. 1:2)

1032. What is the full name of 1 Peter?

1033. What is the full name of 1 John?

1034. How many Epistles did Paul write to the Ephesians?

1035. 2 Thessalonians was written from what city?

Solution on page 278

```
F  R  H  V  V  D  T  D  C  S  Y  K
Y  Y  O  N  K  T  B  L  A  J  S  T
M  F  M  M  I  L  Q  R  M  R  G  W
P  R  K  X  E  C  H  L  E  R  Y  O
H  M  T  F  T  P  O  G  M  Y  J  L
I  R  L  R  A  M  N  P  H  W  L  D
L  N  M  P  J  A  S  T  O  O  N  E
I  L  E  Q  R  U  O  N  L  L  Q  M
P  N  M  T  I  M  L  N  Y  R  I  V
P  Z  S  A  I  M  A  T  H  E  N  S
I  L  G  T  N  L  M  N  L  M  Q  X
E  P  A  P  H  R  O  D  I  T  U  S
```

- John directed his third Epistle to this person. (3 John 1:1)

- How many Epistles did Paul write to the Hebrews?

- The Book of Ephesians was written from this city. (See citation at end of Epistle.)

- Paul wrote this number of Epistles to the Thessalonians.

- Who was a fellow prisoner with Paul when he wrote to Philemon? (Philem. 1:23)

- Paul felt it necessary to send this disciple to the Philippians. (Philip. 2:25)

- The Epistle to Titus was written from this city. (See citation at end of Epistle.)

- 1 Corinthians was written from this city. (See citation at end of Epistle)

  (a) Rome
  (b) Philippi
  (c) Jerusalem

- This person was the companion with Paul when he wrote to Philemon. (Philem. 1:1)

  (a) Timothy
  (b) Barnabus
  (c) Peter

- 1 Thessalonians was written from this city. (See citation at end of Epistle)

- Peter addressed his first Epistle to whom? (1 Pet. 1:1)

  (a) Paul
  (b) the church
  (c) strangers

1084. Paul said that scripture was profitable for what four things (name one)? (2 Tim. 3:16)

1085. Which scripture states that Jesus did not baptize people?

1086. Paul states that the scriptures were given "that the man of God may be" what? (2 Tim. 3:17)

1087. Peter states that we do this to the scriptures, to our destruction. (2 Pet. 3:16)

1088. The Ethiopian eunuch was reading what Old Testament book when Philip joined him? (Acts 8:28)

1089. What Old Testament book did Luke say Jesus read from in the Synagogue in Nazareth when He announced his Messiahship? (Luke 4:17–21)

1090. What did the Jews think the scriptures "gave" them? (John 5:39)

1091. Jesus told the Jews that the scriptures testified of whom? (John 5:39)

1092. Paul, quoting the Psalms, said that man was made a little lower than whom? (Heb. 2:7)

1093. John wrote in Revelation that no one should add to or subtract from his what? (Rev. 22:18–19)

1094. What miracle is found in John 11?

1095. According to Paul, all scripture is given from God by what? (2 Tim. 3:16)

1096. According to Peter, no prophecy of the scripture is of any private what? (2 Pet. 1:20)

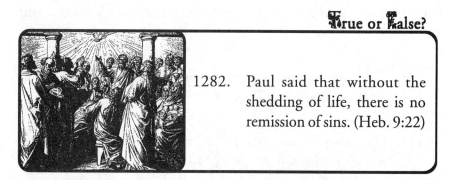

1282. Paul said that without the shedding of life, there is no remission of sins. (Heb. 9:22)

Geography

VIII

1097. Paul declares to the Romans that we should not be conformed to the what? (Rom. 12:2)

1098. What is the name of the well where Jesus spoke to the woman of Samaria? (John 4:6)

1099. What is the name of the hill Paul preached from in Athens? (Acts 17:22)

1100. The Rulers said that no what, had come from Galilee? (John 7:52)

1101. Who came before Jesus, preaching in the wilderness of Judea? (Matt. 3:1)

1102. The Pool of Bethesda was located by what market? (John 5:2)

1103. If all Jesus did was written down, what could not contain the books? (John 21:25)

1104. What area did Jesus depart into after the imprisonment of John the Baptist? (Matt. 4:12)

1105. What was the name of the pool where the impotent man was healed? (John 5:2)

1106. John records that after Jesus left Judea for Galilee, He performed His second miracle when He healed the son of whom? (John 4:49–54)

1107. Some questioned if the Christ could come out of what province? (John 7:41)

1108. Where did the resurrected Jesus tell the women to have the Apostles meet Him? (Matt. 28:10)

1109. What is the main geographical area of Christ's ministry as described by the Synoptics? (*"Synoptics" and "Synoptic Gospels" are common names for the books of Matthew, Mark, and Luke when referred to as a group.*)

1110. What is another name for the Potter's field where Judas hanged himself? (Matt. 27:8)

1111. Paul declared that the earth is the Lord's, and the what thereof? (1 Cor. 10:26)

1112. What is the name of the place near Salim where John the Baptist baptized because there was "much water" there? (John 3:23)

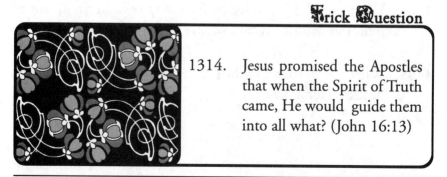

Trick Question

1314. Jesus promised the Apostles that when the Spirit of Truth came, He would guide them into all what? (John 16:13)

1113. Jesus said that after His death the Apostles would weep, but the world would what? (John 16:20)

1114. Jesus prayed not to take the Apostles from the world, but to keep them from what? (John 17:15)

1115. Who does Paul say will judge the world? (1 Cor. 6:2)

1116. By one man, what entered into the world, thereby bringing death to all men? (Rom. 5:12)

1117. If you love the world, whose love is not in you? (1 John 2:15)

1118. What does it profit you if you gain the whole world and lose your own what? (Matt. 16:26)

1119. According to Paul, the sorrow of the world worketh what? (2 Cor. 7:10)

1120. How much did Paul state we brought into this world? (1 Tim. 6:7)

1121. Jesus said He was the what, of the world? (John 8:12)

1122. Paul said that the wisdom of the world is what with God? (1 Cor. 3:19)

1123. Because iniquity shall abound before the end of the world, the love of many shall do what? (Matt. 24:12)

1124. Peter stated that before the foundation of the world, Jesus had been what? (1 Pet. 1:20)

1125. Jesus said that in Him the Apostles would have peace, but in the world they would have what? (John 16:33)

1126. Paul said we were what, before the foundation of the world? (Eph. 1:4)

1127. Jesus said the Apostles would have what because of Him, but while in the world, they would have tribulation? (John 16:33)

True or False?

1283. Paul declares that patience is produced by tribulation, and therefore we should glory in it. (Rom. 5:3)

1128. Peter states that Jesus is a stone of stumbling and a rock of what? (1 Pet. 2:8)

1129. Which Apostle was stoned at Iconium? (Acts 14:19)

1130. Who is the chief corner stone of the church? (Eph. 2:20)

1131. What did the demonic, whose name was Legion, do to himself with stones? (Mark 5:5)

1132. Who was the first disciple to be stoned after the resurrection? (Acts 7:55–60)

1133. Who was the spiritual Rock of the Old Testament? (1 Cor. 10:4)

1134. What did John the Baptist say God could raise up from stones? (Matt. 3:9)

1135. What did Martha say about Lazarus when Jesus told her to have the stone removed from Lazarus' tomb? (John 11:39)

1136. What did the stone which the builders rejected become? (Matt. 21:42)

1137. When they brought the adulteress to Jesus, what did He say her accusers must be before they could cast the first stone? (John 8:7)

1138. Who rolled the stone away from the door of Christ's tomb? (Matt. 28:2)

1139. The Jews could discern the face of the sky, and knew that when the evening sky was red, the weather would be what? (Matt. 16:2)

1140. What did the sound of the rushing wind fill on Pentecost? (Acts 2:2)

1141. Foul weather will come in the morning when the sky is red and what? (Matt. 16:3)

1142. What entity stood by Paul when he was aboard a ship during a storm? (Acts 27:23)

1143. What was Jesus doing when a tempest arose on the sea and threatened the ship He sailed on? (Matt. 8:24)

1144. He that wavereth is like a wave of the sea, driven by what? (James 1:6)

1145. What was the Apostles' initial reaction when Jesus calmed the sea? (Matt. 8:27)

1146. What was the cause of Peter's fear as he walked on the water? (Matt. 14:30)

1147. In John the Revelator's vision, what is the weight of the hailstones in the last plague? (Rev. 16:21)

1148. What occurred after Jesus rebuked the wind and the sea? (Matt. 8:26)

1149. What was the length of time Elias stopped the rain? (James 5:17)

1150. What are the three elements which beat upon the house that was built upon the sand? (Matt. 7:27)

1151. What is the name of the tempestuous wind that beset Paul's voyage? (Acts 27:14)

1152. What are the three elements which beat upon the house built upon the rock? (Matt. 7:25)

1153. The Jews could discern the face of the sky, but could not discern the what, of the times? (Matt. 16:3)

1154. Foul weather will come in the morning when the sky is lowering and what color? (Matt. 16:3)

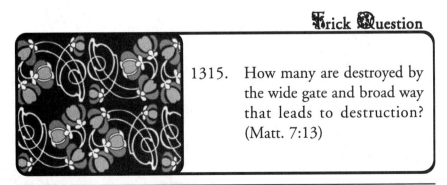

Trick Question

1315. How many are destroyed by the wide gate and broad way that leads to destruction? (Matt. 7:13)

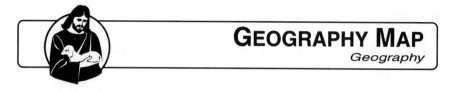

GEOGRAPHY MAP
Geography

Fill in the geographic names for the cities and areas shown below. Use the questions on page 249 to help you.

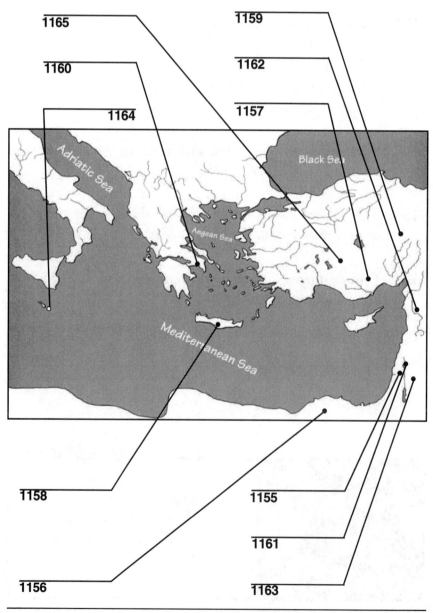

1155. The city of Cana was in what province? (John 4:46)

1156. Where did Joseph take Mary and the baby Jesus in order to avoid Herod? (Matt. 2:13)

1157. Tarsus was a city in what country? (Acts 21:39)

1158. Paul said he had left Titus on what island? (Titus 1:4–5)

1159. The seven churches in Revelation were located on what continent? (Rev. 1:4)

1160. Dionysius the Areopagite was the only male convert identified by name from what city? (Acts 17:22, 34)

1161. What does John state is another name for the Sea of Galilee? (John 6:1)

1162. The area North of Palestine was known as what? (Matt. 4:24)

1163. Jesus saw a small man sitting in a tree trying to see Him as He passed out of what city? (Luke 19:1–5)

1164. After Paul escaped a shipwreck, he found himself on what island? (Acts 28:1)

1165. After Paul and Barnabas shook the dust from their feet against Antioch, they went to what city? (Acts 13:14, 51)

1166. Approximately what distance lies between Bethany and Jerusalem? (John 11:18)

1167. Because of the wise men's visit, Herod and all Jerusalem were what? (Matt. 2:1–3)

1168. What was "strawed" before Jesus as He entered Jerusalem? (Matt. 21:8)

1169. The new Jerusalem will have no need for what two heavenly bodies to provide its light? (Rev. 21:23)

1170. Jesus was riding on a colt as He departed from what city to make His final entrance into Jerusalem? (Matt. 21:1–5)

1171. In John the Revelator's vision, how many horsemen are in the great army? (Rev. 9:16)

1172. What was Jesus called by the multitude as He entered Jerusalem the last time? (Matt. 21:10–11)

1173. Paul went to Jerusalem the second time after how many years? (Gal. 2:1)

1174. What did the people in Jerusalem throw into the air when Paul testified to them? (Acts 22:23)

1175. Jesus said to swear not by Jerusalem, for it is the city of the great what? (Matt. 5:34–35)

1176. What was spread before Jesus when He made his final entry into Jerusalem? (Matt. 21:8)

1177. From what source will the New Jerusalem receive its light? (Rev. 21:23)

1178. Paul finally said that after Jerusalem, he must see what place? (Acts 19:21)

1179. Rather than return to Jerusalem for trial, Paul appealed to whom? (Acts 25:11)

1180. When Jesus entered Jerusalem the people cried out. What was the first word in their cry? (Matt. 21:9)

True or False?

1284. Paul declares that ridiculous and unlearned questions gender strife. (2 Tim. 2:23)

CITY WORD SEARCH

Geography

Solution on page 276

A	Z	O	T	U	S	T	H	Y	A	T	I	R	A	H
L	E	J	E	R	U	S	A	L	E	M	F	Y	K	S
X	R	P	J	B	E	T	H	S	A	I	D	A	I	A
D	Q	K	H	K	N	T	L	F	K	C	N	L	I	T
A	P	W	K	R	K	X	H	Y	N	J	O	H	S	N
M	L	Y	D	D	A	T	K	R	X	P	P	N	N	K
A	N	D	M	L	N	I	H	N	A	L	E	M	C	B
S	F	X	R	I	Z	S	M	C	E	H	U	N	A	E
C	F	J	R	R	U	N	E	D	T	A	L	A	E	T
U	S	O	J	S	P	D	A	A	N	P	Q	Z	S	H
S	C	Y	R	M	O	L	N	R	V	W	B	A	A	A
V	K	A	C	N	I	D	E	C	L	K	R	R	R	N
Y	T	T	M	H	A	P	O	X	A	T	B	E	E	Y
C	L	Y	P	W	A	I	T	M	Y	N	L	T	A	N
X	T	T	T	C	N	R	N	B	Q	J	A	H	T	B

- This is the name of the lake coast city where Jesus dwelt after leaving Nazareth. (Matt. 4:13)

- A devout man named Simeon was in this city when he praised the baby Jesus. (Luke 2:25)

- Jesus went to this place to avoid the Jewish leadership after raising Lazarus from the dead. (John 11:54)

  (a) Capernaum
  (b) Bethlehem
  (c) Ephraim

- Nathanael questioned if any good thing could come from this city when he was told of Jesus. (John 1:46)

- Damaris was the only female convert identified by name from this city. (Acts 17:22, 34)

  (a) Athens
  (b) Corinth
  (c) Jerusalem

- Tabitha was raised from the dead in this city. (Acts 9:38, 40)

- Saul was from this city. (Acts 9:11)

- The City of Jerusalem is called by the name "Egypt" and what city's name in the book of Revelation? (Rev. 11:8)

- Saul desired letters of authority to the synagogues in this city to persecute the saints. (Acts 9:2)

- After being healed, the man cleansed of the demons named "Legion" departed and began to publish "how great things Jesus had done for him" in this city. (Mark 5:20)

  (a) Athens
  (b) Damascus
  (c) Decapolis

- Philip was transported by the Spirit to this city after the baptism of the eunuch. (Acts 8:39–40)

- This was the city of the Samaritan woman who Jesus spoke to by Jacob's well. (John 4:5)

- Philip, one of the seven, lived in this city. (Acts 21:8)

- This is the name of one of the seven churches in Revelation. It is also the same of a major city in Pennsylvania. (Rev. 1:11)

- Lydia was converted to the gospel in this city. (Acts 16:14–15)

- This is the name of the city where Jesus raised the widow's son from the dead. (Luke 7:11, 15)

- This is the name of the town of Mary, Martha, and Lazarus. (John 11:1)

- The Apostle Philip was from this city. (John 1:44)

  (a) Bethany
  (b) Nazareth
  (c) Bethsaida

- The Lord spoke to Paul and told him to stay in this city. (Acts 18:1, 10–11)

  (a) Caesarea
  (b) Tarsus
  (c) Corinth

- Jesus attended a marriage celebration in this city. (John 2:1)

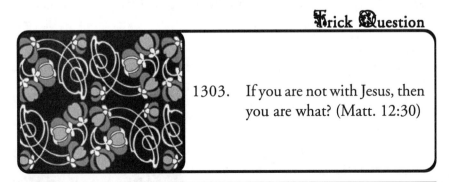

🍂rick 🍂uestion

1303. If you are not with Jesus, then you are what? (Matt. 12:30)

1181. What heavenly things did Paul say no man should worship? (Col. 2:18)

1182. What will fall from heaven before Christ's coming? (Matt. 24:29)

    a.   the stars
    b.   the moon
    c.   the comets

1183. The Father makes the sun to rise upon both the good and the what? (Matt. 5:45)

1184. Which Apostle was called "Jupiter?" (Acts 14:12)

1185. In the day of the Lord, what shall pass away with great noise? (2 Pet. 3:10)

1186. Paul compared the glory of resurrected bodies to what three heavenly things? (1 Cor. 15:41)

1187. What will be darkened in the heavens before Christ's Second Coming? (Matt. 24:29)

Nations

IX

1218. The blessings of Abraham comes to the Gentiles through whom? (Gal. 3:14)

1219. What Gentile was told to send for Peter because of a vision? (Acts 10:1)

1220. What military rank did Cornelius hold? (Acts 10:22)

1221. Matthew states that the Centurion's servant had what disease? (Matt. 8:6)

1222. What did Peter observe was poured out upon Cornelius? (Acts 10:45)

1223. How long did the Ephesians cry, "Great is Diana of the Ephesians," in opposition to Paul? (Acts 19:34)

1224. Which Jewish sect demanded that converted Gentiles be circumcised and keep the Law of Moses? (Acts 15:5)

1225. Who does Luke say the centurion sent to entreat Jesus to heal his servant? (Luke 7:3)

1226. What people (nationality) forbid Paul to speak to the Gentiles? (1 Thes. 2:14, 16)

1227. What did Cornelius do when he first met Peter? (Acts 10:25)

1228. What Roman soldier asked Jesus to heal his servant? (Matt. 8:5)

1229. Who was the Apostle sent to the Gentiles? (Rom. 11:13)

1230. The Centurion asked Jesus to heal his servant with only a what? (Matt. 8:8)

NATIONS CROSSWORD
Nations

Solution on page 288

Across

1   This was the name of the wife of Chuza. (Luke 8:3)

6   This is the number of people that were killed when the tower at Siloam fell on them. (Luke 13:4)

7   Paul said that Hymenaeus and Philetus taught that this event had already taken place. (2 Tim. 2:17–18)

9   1 Timothy was written from this city.

10 This is the gospel that is not included in the term "Synoptics."

11 These are the last two words at the end of the New Testament.

13 The people at Lystra gave Paul this name. (Acts 14:12)

15 Drusilla, the wife of Felix, was of this nationality. (Acts 24:24)

17 This is the number of Epistles James wrote.

18 This was Paul's companion when he wrote 1 Corinthians. (1 Cor. 1:1)

19 The Spirit (or word of God) is this part of the armor of God. (Eph. 6:17)

23 Paul said that mysteries were made known to him by this means. (Eph. 3:3)

24 This is the first book in the New Testament.

26 This was the name of the orator brought by the Jews to testify against Paul. (Acts 24:1)

27 Melchizedek blessed this person when he met him coming from the slaughter of the kings. (Heb. 7:1)

30 This was the companion with Paul when he wrote to the Philippians (another spelling for Timothy). (Philip. 1:1)

31 As John introduces the book of Revelation, he states that the things he will describe will come to pass at this time. (Rev. 1:1)

Down

2 This is the last word in the book of Jude.

3 This is the name of the street where Ananias was told to go to find Saul and heal him. (Acts 9:11)

4 This is the number of books in the New Testament that John wrote.

5 Paul declared that he was a descendant from this tribe of Israel. (Philip. 3:5)

8 Peter said we should add this to our virtue. (2 Pet. 1:5)

12 This was Paul's companion when he wrote 2 Corinthians. (2 Cor. 1:1)

14 The Book of Romans was written from this city.

16 2 Corinthians was written from this city.

20 This was the goddess of the Ephesians. (Acts 19:34)

21 This was the trade of Demetrius at Ephesus. (Acts 19:24)

22 This is the country where the letter to the Hebrews was written (postscript to the letter).

25 Peter said we should add this to our brotherly kindness. (2 Pet. 1:7)

28 After their contention over missionary companions, Paul and Barnabus split up. Who took Silas? (Acts 15:40)

29 This is the number of Epistles Paul wrote to Timothy.

1188. To whom did James address his Epistle? (James 1:1)

1189. What is the single scriptural reference that tells of Jesus' growth from age twelve to adulthood?

1190. What should we lay up for ourselves in heaven? (Matt. 6:20)

1191. What is the interpretation of the word, "Talithacumi"? (Mark 5:41)

1192. James was written from what location?

1193. What did John say was the name of the Jewish feast that Jesus went up to in secret? (John 7:2, 10)

1194. What was the Samaritan woman's declaration (the woman by the well) when Jesus told her of her past? (John 4:19)

1195. Paul said that the Spirit itself beareth witness with our what? (Rom. 8:16)

1196. Who was the only male convert in Athens that was identified specifically by name? (Acts 17:34)

1197. In which chapter in 1 Corinthians does Paul deal with spiritual gifts?

1198. The kingdom is hidden from the wise and prudent and revealed to whom? (Matt. 11:25)

1199. What chapter in Galatians lists the works of the flesh?

1200. What book, chapter, and verse contain the golden rule?

1201. What chapter in Colossians recites Paul's instructions to "put off" and "put on" various attributes?

1202. What chapter in Romans directs us to obey governments?

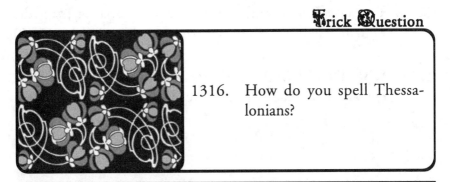

Trick Question

1316. How do you spell Thessalonians?

1203. What was the name of the Jewish celebration Jesus kept the night of His arrest? (Matt. 26:18)

1204. Whose houses did Jesus say the Pharisees devoured? (Matt. 23:14)

1205. What concept of the Jewish rulers made God's word of "none effect"? (Mark 7:13)

1206. Why did John say that Jesus would not walk in "Jewry"? (John 7:1)

1207. What did the Pharisees make broad to be seen of men? (Matt. 23:5)

1208. The Pharisees heard that Jesus had put what religious group to silence? (Matt. 22:34)

1209. Paul declared that the Jews always require a what? (1 Cor. 1:22)

1210. The Jewish rulers said that if all men believed in Jesus, the Romans would come and take what two things? (John 11:48)

1211. What did the Jews think that Jesus would do to Himself when He said they could not go where He was going? (John 8:22)

1212. Jesus told the Jews that the scriptures testify of whom? (John 5:39)

1213. Because Jesus came, the Jews had no "cloak" for their what? (John 15:22)

1214. Paul said that to the Jews, Christ was a what? (1 Cor. 1:23)

1215. What Jewish political group joined with the Pharisees to destroy Jesus? (Mark 3:6)

1216. The Jews initially claimed their father was Abraham, then said they had but one Father, even who? (John 8:41)

1217. Which person did the Jews believe was healed in the pool of Bethesda after the water moved? (John 5:4)

JEWS WORD SEARCH
Nations

Solution on page 283

T	B	L	L	B	D	I	R	K	S	N	K	N
H	H	R	X	H	B	R	H	U	G	T	R	V
E	H	L	J	B	Z	W	E	I	L	P	D	I
S	Y	H	A	D	M	H	S	N	M	X	S	P
S	D	R	D	Z	T	A	E	C	L	K	C	E
A	B	P	C	O	A	R	V	M	H	H	R	R
L	M	R	M	K	D	R	Y	W	J	T	I	S
O	M	I	M	L	R	Q	U	R	B	Y	P	Y
N	T	O	I	X	G	O	D	S	F	Y	T	H
I	Z	H	S	K	V	Y	H	O	N	O	U	R
C	C	M	N	E	F	L	M	M	L	L	R	X
A	L	M	D	D	S	T	X	N	K	C	E	T
D	V	H	K	K	M	D	E	V	I	L	S	N

- Because of the Jews, Paul circumcised this companion (whose father was a Greek). (Acts 16:1, 3)

- After the Jews boasted that Abraham was their father, Jesus said their real father was the what? (John 8:44)

- The Jews told the blind man healed by Jesus that they were not disciples of Jesus, but disciples of this man. (John 9:28)

- Jesus told the Jews to search these for they testified of Him. (John 5:39)

- Jesus said the scribes and the Pharisees loved men to call them by this title. (Matt. 23:7)

- Jesus chided the Jews for seeking this from each other, and not from God. (John 5:44)

- The Jewish leadership was angry when many people believed on Jesus because of the raising of this friend. (John 12:10–11)

- John the Baptist called the Pharisees and Sadducees a generation of these. (Matt. 3:7)

- The Jewish leaders requested multiple times that Jesus show them one of these. (Matt. 12:38)

- The Jews accepted the responsibility for Jesus' death by telling Pilate: "His blood be on us, and on our _____." (Matt. 27:25)

- The Jews accused Jesus of making Himself this person. (John 10:33)

- Jews from this city went to Berea to oppress Paul. (Acts 17:13)

Challenged by the New Testament

1231. Which two were sent with Paul and Barnabus to Antioch? (Acts 15:22)

1232. Name one of the two men called a "canker" by Paul in 2 Timothy? (2 Tim. 2:17)

1233. The second James of the Apostles was the son of whom? (Matt. 10:3)

1234. Which two companions were with Paul when he wrote to the Thessalonians? (1: Thes. 1:1)

1235. What is another name of Elymas the sorcerer? (Acts 13:6, 8)

1236. What is the name of the father of Levi who sat at custom when Jesus said, "follow me"? (Mark 2:14)

1237. Who did not open the door of the gate for Peter when he knocked, after he had been released from prison by angels? (Acts 12:13–14)

1238. What was the name of the Greek/Ephesian Paul took with him into the Temple? (Acts 21:28–29)

1239. What is the name of the Caiaphas' father-in-law? (John 18:13)

1240. What Jew from Alexandria eloquently taught only John's baptism in Ephesus? (Acts 18:24–25)

1241. What was the name of the only identified female convert in Athens? (Acts 17:34)

1242. What was the name of the Centurion Paul was delivered to and who took him to Rome? (Acts 27:1)

1243. What was Simon's (the chief Apostle's), other name? (Matt. 10:2)

1244. Paul, on Melita, healed the father of what man? (Acts 28:8)

1245. Who is the brother of Jesus whose name begins with S? (Matt. 13:55)

1246. Paul sent what disciple to the Thessalonians? (1 Thes. 3:2)

1247. What was the first name of Pilate? (Matt. 27:2)

1248. What was the surname of Barsabas who was considered to replace Judas? (Acts 1:23)

1249. What is the "interpretation" of the name Tabitha? (Acts 9:36)

1250. What is the interpretation of the name "Aceldama?" (Acts 1:19)

1251. What was the surname of Judas, the companion to Paul and Barnabus? (Acts 15:22)

1252. Mark said Jesus gave what surname to James and John? (Mark 3:17)

1253. When Paul and Barnabus split up as missionaries, Paul took which companion? (Acts 15:40)

1254. The Apostle Judas (not Iscariot) had two other names, what were they? (Matt. 10:3; Mark 3:18; Luke 6:16; John 14:22)

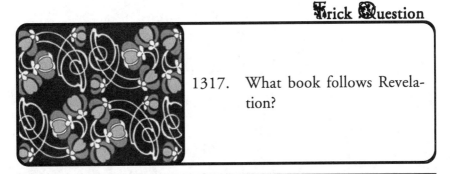

Trick Question

1317. What book follows Revelation?

One of the most interesting characters in the New Testament is John the Baptist. Because of his unique mission as the forerunner of the Son of God, he plays an important role in the Gospels. However, when his witness concludes at the baptism of Jesus, his importance diminishes in the scriptural text. He is arrested, and languishes in prison for over a year before his death. There are multiple questions concerning John throughout this book and a specific heading for him, but it is his death that draws our attention here. Herodias, the adulterous wife of Herod Antipas, had long desired the death of John. On the occasion of Herod's birthday celebration, the daughter of Herodias danced for Herod and his guests. Herod was so entranced by her that he offered her anything she desired as a reward, up to one-half of his kingdom. After consulting with her mother, the girl requested the head of John the Baptist in a charger—which Herod provided because of his oath. That leads us to the final question:

1285. If the daughter of Herodias (who danced for Herod and received the head of John the Baptist in a charger) is identified by name in the New Testament, give her name.

Look up this interesting answer in the Answer Section.

Surprised?

You started your trek into the New Testament with a question and an answer. I'll share one more interesting question and answer with you as we conclude. There are three names in the New Testament for the fresh water lake that feeds the Jordan River, and a fourth, different name, in the Old Testament.

Question: Can you list the four names used to identify the fresh water sea that feeds the Jordan river?

Answer: The Sea of Chinnereth (Num. 34:11)
The Sea of Galilee (Matt. 4:18)
The Lake of Gennesaret (Luke 5:1)
and The Sea of Tiberias (John 6:1).

I hope you've had as much fun answering these questions as I had in preparing them. If you have read and answered every question, congratulations! Especially if you can remember the answers!

Some people today question the Divinity of Jesus Christ, but I cannot read the New Testament without concluding that those who wrote the text knew Jesus was the Son of God and the sole means by which salvation can be attained in God's Kingdom. However, the Savior leaves it up to each individual to determine whether he or she will accept Him and believe on His words. So thanks to Matthew, Mark, Luke, John, Paul, James, Peter, Jude, and all their associates for giving us their witness of Him. And thanks to the Messiah for His sacrifice and for caring enough to provide the way for us to follow.

And a special thanks to God for loving us so much, "that he gave his only begotten Son, that whosoever believeth in him should not perish, but have everlasting life."

— *E. Keith Howick*

Answers

PUZZLE SOLUTIONS

About People Word Search

from page 38

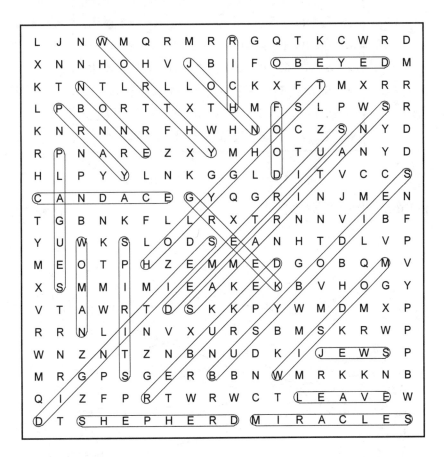

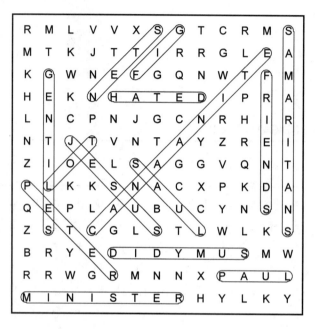

Baptism Match Game   from page 126

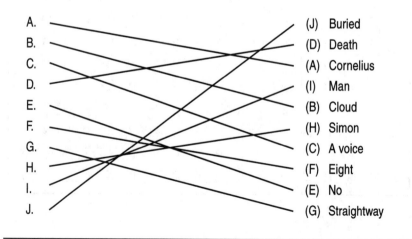

A.
B.
C.
D.
E.
F.
G.
H.
I.
J.

(J) Buried
(D) Death
(A) Cornelius
(I) Man
(B) Cloud
(H) Simon
(C) A voice
(F) Eight
(E) No
(G) Straightway

Body Parts Crossword

from page 102

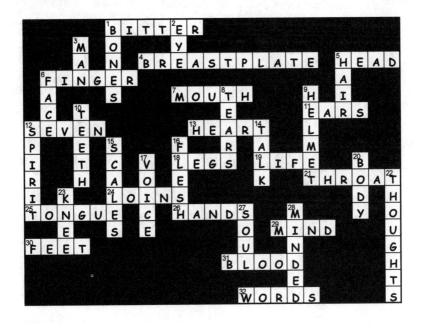

Body Parts Word Search

from page 202

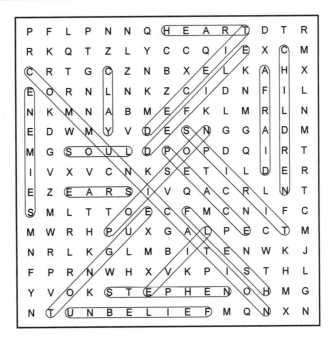

Church Crossword

from page 190

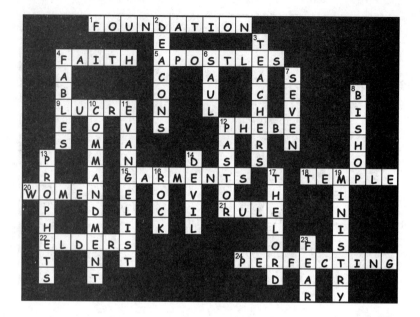

City Word Search

from page 252

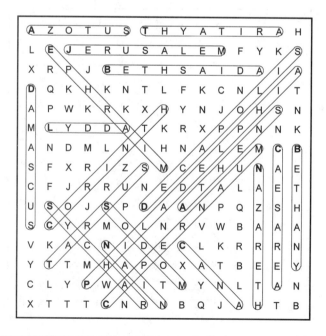

Challenged by the New Testament

Definitions Crossword

from page 128

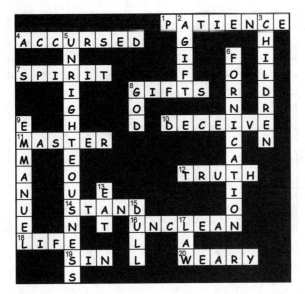

Doctrine Crossword

from page 112

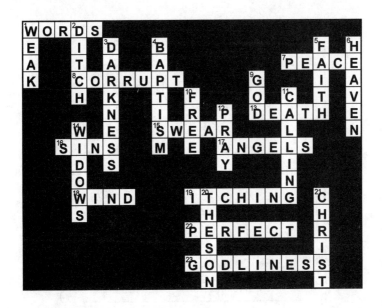

Easy Trivia Word Search

from page 106

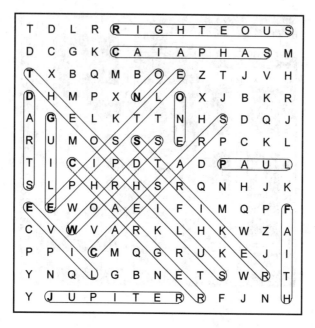

Epistles Trivia Word Search

from page 236

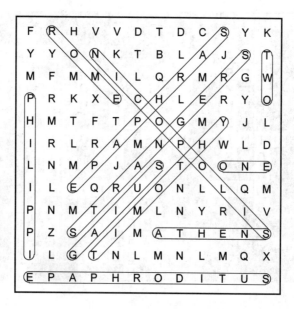

Challenged by the New Testament

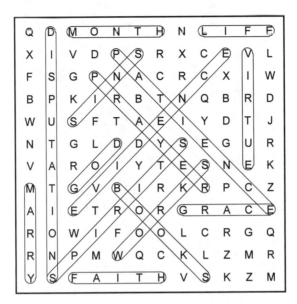

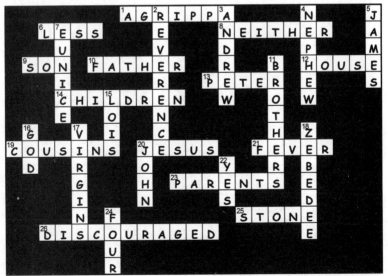

6 Across: James the Less is the name traditionally given by Biblical scholars to Jude the Apostle.

Family and Fellow Man Word Search

from page 171

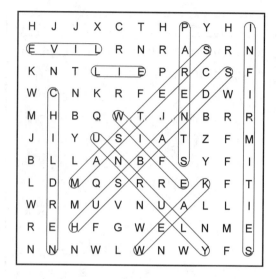

Food and Drink Word Search

from page 164

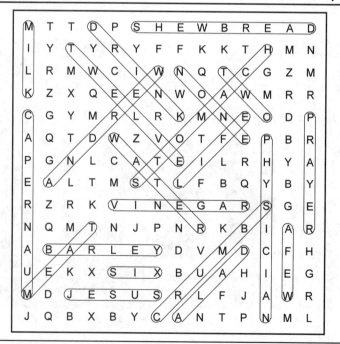

Challenged by the New Testament

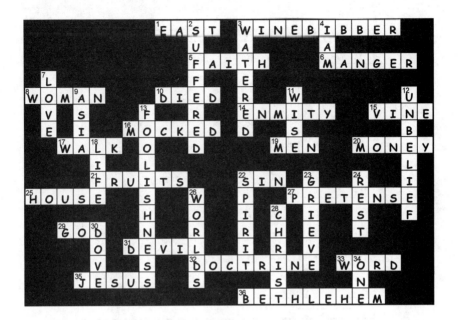

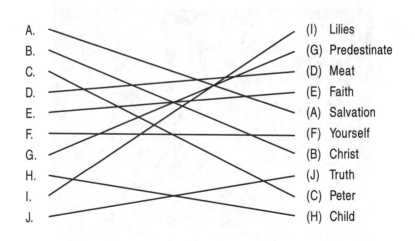

A.
B.
C.
D.
E.
F.
G.
H.
I.
J.

(I) Lilies
(G) Predestinate
(D) Meat
(E) Faith
(A) Salvation
(F) Yourself
(B) Christ
(J) Truth
(C) Peter
(H) Child

Imagery Word Search

from page 88

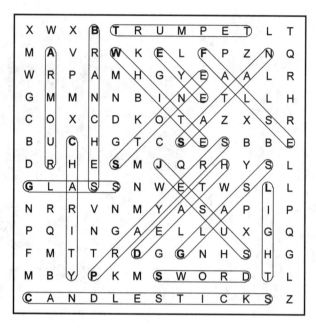

Instructions and Goals Crossword

from page 132

Challenged by the New Testament

Jews Word Search
from page 264

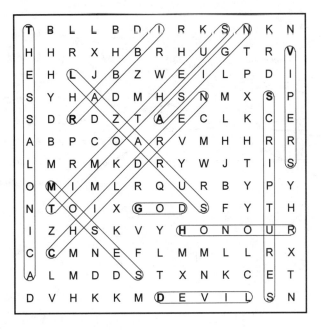

John the Baptist Crossword
from page 44

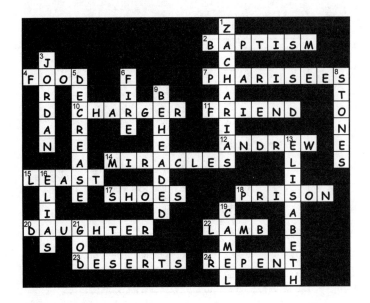

John's Vision Match Game

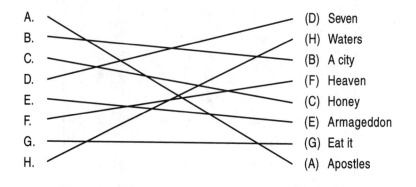

A.	(D) Seven
B.	(H) Waters
C.	(B) A city
D.	(F) Heaven
E.	(C) Honey
F.	(E) Armageddon
G.	(G) Eat it
H.	(A) Apostles

Judas Iscariot Word Search

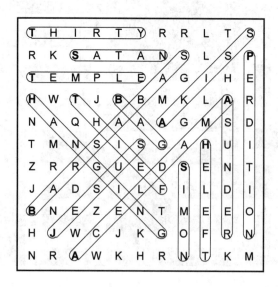

Challenged by the New Testament

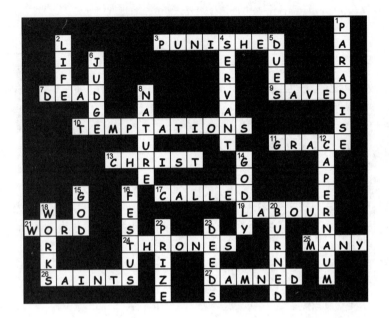

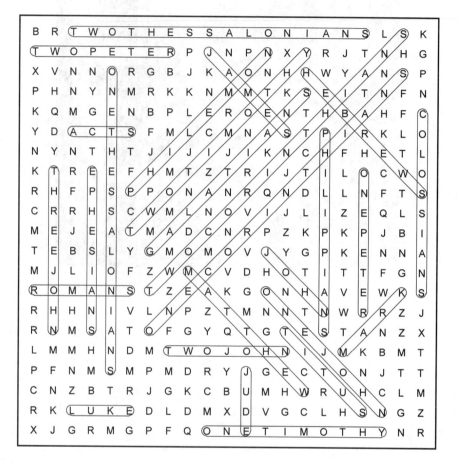

Know Your Books Crossword

from page 230

The Law Crossword

from page 124

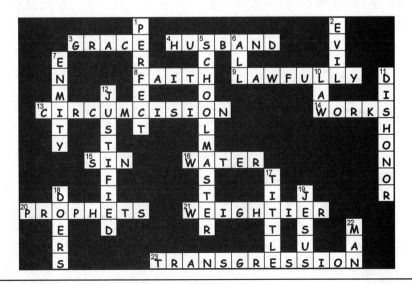

Nations Crossword

from page 258

Men Match Game #1

from page 61

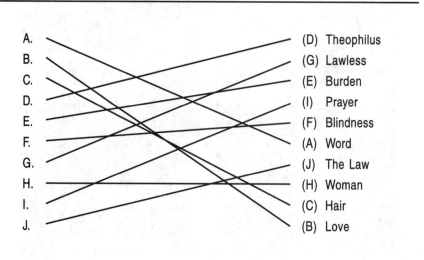

A.
B.
C.
D.
E.
F.
G.
H.
I.
J.

(D) Theophilus
(G) Lawless
(E) Burden
(I) Prayer
(F) Blindness
(A) Word
(J) The Law
(H) Woman
(C) Hair
(B) Love

Challenged by the New Testament

Men Match Game #2

from page 77

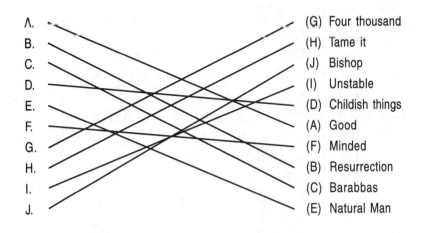

A.
B.
C.
D.
E.
F.
G.
H.
I.
J.

(G) Four thousand
(H) Tame it
(J) Bishop
(I) Unstable
(D) Childish things
(A) Good
(F) Minded
(B) Resurrection
(C) Barabbas
(E) Natural Man

Miracles Crossword

from page 162

Miracles Word Search

from page 158

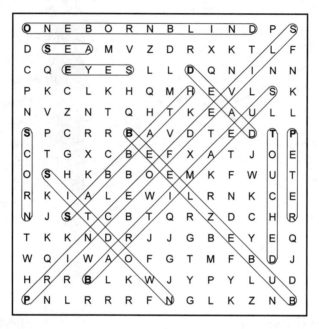

Names Word Search

from page 78

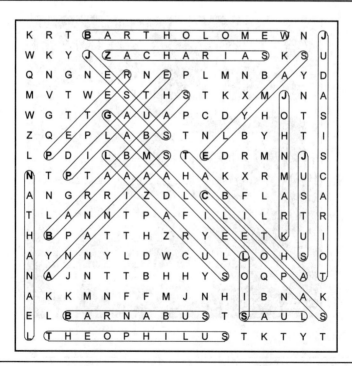

Challenged by the New Testament

Parables Crossword

from page 182

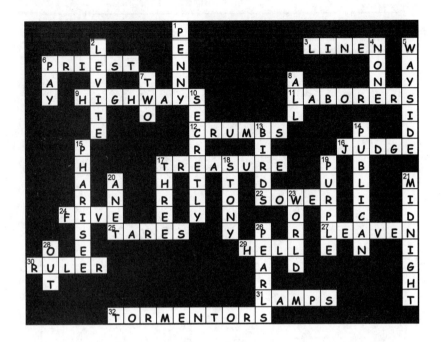

Parables Word Search

from page 180

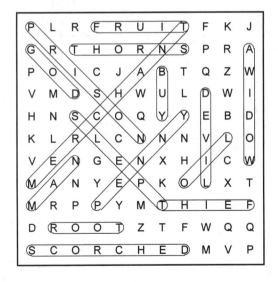

Paul Word Search

from page 54

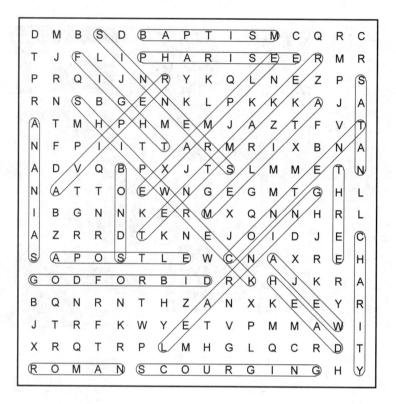

Peter Match Game

from page 46

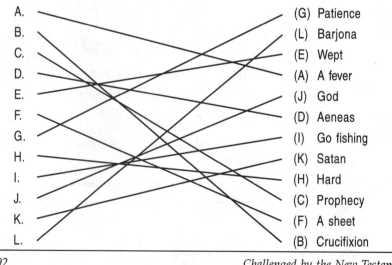

A.
B.
C.
D.
E.
F.
G.
H.
I.
J.
K.
L.

(G) Patience
(L) Barjona
(E) Wept
(A) A fever
(J) God
(D) Aeneas
(I) Go fishing
(K) Satan
(H) Hard
(C) Prophecy
(F) A sheet
(B) Crucifixion

Resurrection Crossword

from page 30

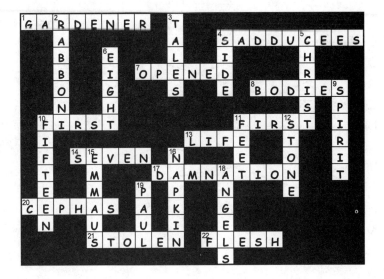

Revelator's Imagery Crossword, The

from page 50

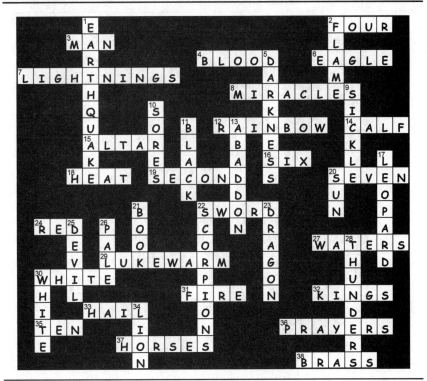

Rulers Match Game

from page 72

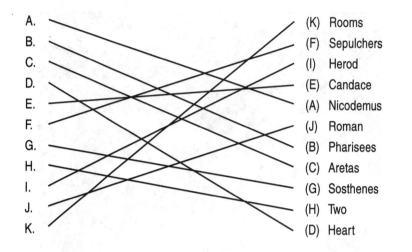

A.
B.
C.
D.
E.
F.
G.
H.
I.
J.
K.

(K) Rooms
(F) Sepulchers
(I) Herod
(E) Candace
(A) Nicodemus
(J) Roman
(B) Pharisees
(C) Aretas
(G) Sosthenes
(H) Two
(D) Heart

Satan and Possession Crossword

from page 140

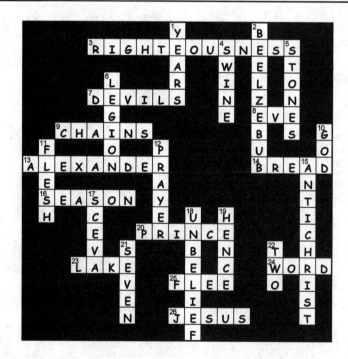

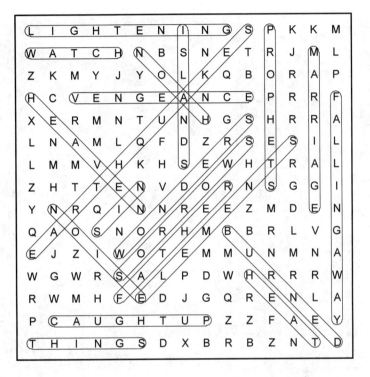

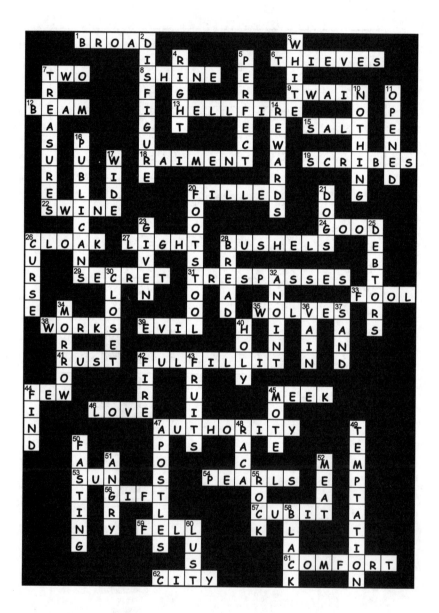

Sermon Word Search, The

from page 150

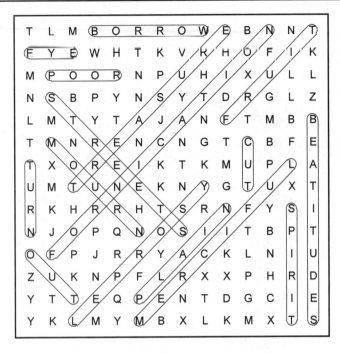

Signs and Visions Crossword

from page 90

Sin Match Game

from page 136

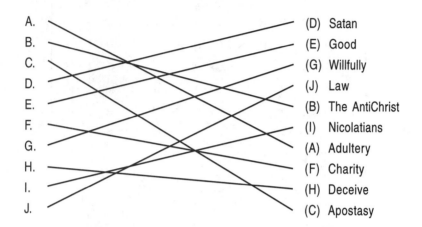

A.
B.
C.
D.
E.
F.
G.
H.
I.
J.

(D) Satan
(E) Good
(G) Willfully
(J) Law
(B) The AntiChrist
(I) Nicolatians
(A) Adultery
(F) Charity
(H) Deceive
(C) Apostasy

Symbolism Crossword

from page 98

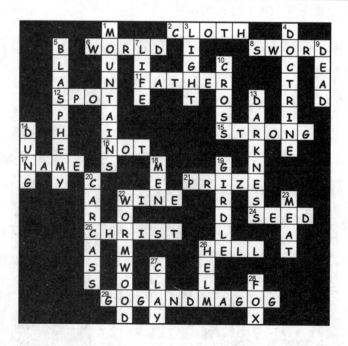

Challenged by the New Testament

Temptations Crossword

from page 16

Unique Fine Points Crossword

from page 184

Women Crossword

from page 62

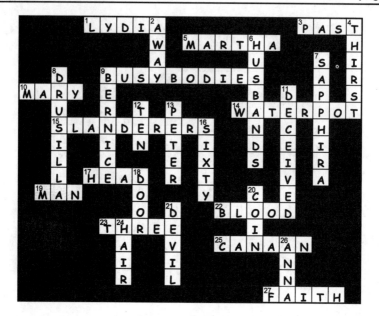

Sin Word Search

from page 138

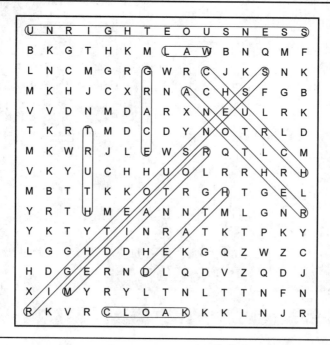

Challenged by the New Testament

NUMBERED QUESTIONS

Answers to True & False questions and Trick Questions can be found near the end of the list.

START

1. At the baptism of Jesus, Matt. 3:17; on the Mt. of Transfiguration, Matt. 17:5; and at His entrance into Jerusalem, John 12:28.

GOD

2. Spirit.
3. Eternal life.
4. "Draw" them.
5. Himself.
6. Confusion.
7. Sinned.
8. Himself.
9. The world.
10. "He which is of God."
11. Faith.
12. "To The Unknown God."
13. The Spirit of God.
14. His only begotten Son.
15. Mediator.
16. The living.
17. The Word.
18. World.
19. The worlds.
20. Perform.

JESUS CHRIST

21. Christ's triumphant entrance into Jerusalem.
22. The Father.
23. "The son of David."
24. The Word.
25. Luke 2:40.
26. They wanted to kill Him.
27. "No man knoweth whence his is.".
28. John Baptist, Elias, or Jeremias.
29. He that came down from heaven.
30. Galilee.
31. An unclean, or evil spirit.
32. They worshiped Him.
33. Force Him to be king.
34. Swaddling clothes.
35. The spirit.
36. "Let the dead bury their dead."
37. The Father.
38. The Son of Man, or Jesus.
39. An angel.
40. The spirit of prophecy.
41. God.
42. Mediator.
43. The Samaritan woman by the well.
44. Shepherds.
45. Gluttonous.

THE HOLY GHOST

46. Sin.
47. The Comforter.
48. Pentecost.
49. Simon the sorcerer.
50. She died.
51. Comforter.
52. By the laying on of hands.

53. The Ethiopian eunuch.

TRANSFIGURATION

54. The Resurrection.
55. Peter, James, and John.
56. Moses and Elias (or Elijah).
57. Three tabernacles.
58. A high mountain.
59. They fell on their face.
60. The Father, or God the Father.
61. A cloud.
62. Like the Sun.

QUESTIONS

63. The Christ.
64. "How knoweth this man letters?"
65. "We cannot tell."
66. Tribute.
67. The temple.
68. Malchus.
69. John the Baptist.
70. Caesar.
71. The Good Samaritan.
72. The resurrection.
73. All the Apostles.

LAST SUPPER

74. They sang a hymn.
75. A towel.
76. Heart.
77. The sacrament.
78. Feet.
79. The Father.
80. Spirit.
81. To love one another.
82. "Lord, Is it I?"
83. The way.
84. Water.
85. Thomas.
86. A sop.
87. The Father.

TRIALS AND ARREST

88. Herod.
89. Caiaphas.

90. Caiaphas.
91. Ananias.
92. Two.
93. Pilate.
94. King Agrippa.
95. He rent his clothes.
96. Spit on Him, buffeted Him, and smote Him.
97. Blasphemy.
98. His ear.
99. Judas Iscariot.
100. High priest.
101. Thorns.

WITNESSES

102. Saul.
103. The gospel.
104. Every word.
105. Works.
106. Jesus Himself, and His Father.
107. Three and one-half days.
108. Olive trees.
109. The beast.
110. The resurrection.
111. The Father, the Word, and the Holy Ghost.
112. Stephen's.
113. Spirit, water, and blood.
114. Not true.

IN THE GARDEN

115. Malchus.
116. Three.
117. Gethsemane.
118. Cedron.
119. A "cup."
120. Judas Iscariot.
121. Peter, James, and John (the two sons of Zebedee).
122. Sleeping.

CRUCIFIXION

123. "This is Jesus the King of the Jews."
124. Blood and water.
125. A place of a skull.

126. Vinegar mixed with gall.
127. Two.
128. He forgave them.
129. Without seam.
130. "I thirst."
131. Simon.
132. Mary Magdalene; Mary the mother of James and Joses; and the mother of James and John (the children of Zebedee).
133. "Father, into thy hands I commend my spirit."
134. The ghost.
135. Scarlet.
136. To remember him in his kingdom.
137. Darkness.
138. "To day shalt thou be with me in paradise."
139. Golgotha.
140. A reed.

ASCENSION

141. Forty.
142. Two.
143. Mount Olivet.
144. "A sabbath day's journey."
145. White.
146. A cloud.
147. The Holy Ghost.

SUFFERING

148. Suffer.
149. God.
150. Persecutions.
151. Evil.
152. Obedience.
153. Charity.

MARY

154. "Wist ye not that I must be about my Father's business?"
155. Espoused to Joseph, engaged, or single.
156. A pair of turtle doves, or two pigeons.

157. Gabriel.
158. Joseph.
159. "Woman."
160. The Holy Ghost.

JOSEPH

161. Through dreams.
162. An angel.
163. To be taxed.
164. A carpenter.
165. A just man.
166. An angel.
167. He wanted to "put her away privily."
168. Mary.
169. Nazareth.

FAMILY TREE

170. Sisters.
171. God.
172. Elisabeth.
173. Mary.
174. James, Simon, Joses, or Judas.
175. John the Baptist.
176. Judah, or Judas.
177. David.
178. Ruth.
179. Joseph.
180. James.
181. Boaz.
182. Jesus.

FUN TREE

183. Zaccaeus.

PETER

184. Brotherly kindness.
185. Fifteen.
186. The Father.
187. "Repent and be baptized."
188. His hands and head.
189. The sick.
190. Turn from it.
191. The uncircumcised.
192. Rebuked Jesus.

193. To come to Him, or to walk on the water also.

JOHN'S VISION

194. The New Jerusalem.
195. Seven.
196. Seven seals.
197. One-half hour.
198. They could not sell merchandise any longer.
199. Things sacrificed to idols.
200. The water of the Euphrates dries up.
201. "Time and times and half a time."
202. The Lord's day.
203. The sixth angel.
204. The seven churches.
205. The Ark of the Testament, or Covenant.
206. Christ, (the Root of David).
207. The sea becomes as the blood of a dead man.
208. A crown of twelve stars.

TIMOTHY

209. The scriptures.
210. Circumcision.
211. Gift.
212. Endless genealogies.
213. His son.
214. Babblings.
215. Blameless.
216. Youth.
217. Fables.

SAUL

218. Kill him.
219. A basket.
220. Gamaliel.
221. "Wasted it."
222. Bar-jesus.
223. Jesus.
224. Barnabas.
225. He was stuck blind.
226. He fasted.

PAUL

227. He would suffer many things.
228. A night and a day.
229. A shipwreck.
230. A dispensation of the gospel.
231. They stoned him.
232. The third heaven.
233. Three.
234. Faith.
235. Satan.
236. Roman.
237. His handkerchiefs, or aprons.
238. Appealed to Caesar.
239. The ministry.
240. Upside down.
241. John Mark.
242. Casting out an evil spirit.
243. They would neither eat nor drink.
244. Three.
245. The gospel of Christ.
246. Life and death.
247. Flesh and blood.

LAZARUS

248. Kill him.
249. He was dead.
250. Two days.
251. Caiaphas.
252. Graveclothes.
253. The glory of God.
254. A napkin.
255. Lazarus, or one from the dead.
256. To Abraham's bosom.
257. Sores.
258. To kill Him.
259. Dogs.
260. Thomas.
261. Lazarus' sisters, or Mary and Martha.

WOMEN

262. Touching Him.
263. Herodias.
264. The man.

265. Modest apparel.
266. Her hair.
267. Tabitha.
268. Precious ointment.
269. Mary Magdalene.
270. Mary.
271. To tempt Him, that they may have cause to accuse Him.
272. 1 Corinthians 11.

HUSBANDS & WIVES

273. World.
274. Unbelievers.
275. Father and mother.
276. Hearts.
277. Put away.
278. The unbelieving husband.
279. Burn.
280. The church.
281. Seven.
282. The weaker vessel.
283. church.
284. Ananias.
285. One.
286. Lamps.
287. He was made dumb.
288. One.

CHILDREN

289. Onesimus.
290. That James and John sit on the right and left hand of Christ in His kingdom.
291. Subjection.
292. A millstone.
293. Light.
294. Two years and under.
295. Predestinated.
296. The peacemakers.
297. Faith.

HERODS

298. None.
299. He slew all male children under two years of age.

300. They were warned in a dream not to.
301. What time the star had appeared.
302. James.
303. He was smitten by an angel.
304. His oath's sake.
305. John the Baptist.

RULERS

306. Nicodemus.
307. Excommunication, or being cast out of the synagogue.
308. Threatened them.
309. In the synagogues.
310. The Holy Ghost.
311. They rejoiced.
312. Herod the King (Herod the Great).
313. Nicodemus.
314. The Pharisees.
315. All.
316. Archelaus.

PILATE

317. He washed his hands.
318. World.
319. A watch, or guards
320. The Praetorium.
321. "What is truth?"
322. A dream.
323. Joseph of Arimathaea.
324. "Art thou the King of the Jews?"
325. He scourged Him.

ALL ABOUT TREES

326. Thorn.
327. The Apostles.
328. Olive tree.
329. Zacchaeus.
330. An axe.
331. Jesus.
332. An olive tree.
333. A sycamore.

NAMES

334. "God with us."

335. A stone.
336. "O Lord," or "thou Son of David."
337. Peter.
338. Peter.
339. Alpha and Omega.
340. The Holy Ghost.
341. The rich fool.
342. Peter.
343. The Prodigal Son.
344. Barnabus.
345. The Sea of Galilee.
346. Leprosy.
347. Bartimaeus.
348. The Passover.

SAINTS

349. Household.
350. Elect.
351. The world.
352. Ignorant.
353. Christians.
354. Tribulation.
355. Priesthood.
356. Widows.
357. Divisions.
358. Paul.
359. Who had baptized them.
360. Fellow citizens.
361. Chloe.
362. The world.
363. Children.

IMAGERY

364. True.
365. Appearance.
366. It withered away and died.
367. Strong meat.
368. The laborers.
369. His Father.
370. A serpent.
371. The branches.
372. The blind.
373. Living water.
374. Garments.
375. Her chickens.

376. Chapter 5 (Gal. 5:22–25).
377. Grass.
378. Before a cock crows he shall deny Jesus three times.

SIGNS AND VISIONS

379. An evil and adulterous one.
380. Things common and unclean, specifically: "four footed beasts, wild beasts, creeping things, and fowls of the air."
381. Abraham.
382. The abomination of desolation.
383. John the Baptist.
384. Abraham's seed.
385. He bound Paul hand and feet.
386. That He took our infirmity and sickness.
387. Abraham.
388. The Holy Ghost.
389. John the Baptist.
390. There would be "hurt and much damage."
391. Abraham.

ANIMALS AND REPTILES

392. Understand.
393. About two thousand.
394. Vipers.
395. The red dragon.
396. Serpents.
397. The lion.
398. They ran into the sea and drowned.
399. The House of Israel.
400. The lost sheep.
401. Sheep.
402. Dogs.
403. The tribute money.
404. The Pharisees and Sadducees.
405. One.
406. Doves.
407. Water, or a flood.
408. The shepherd.
409. Israel.
410. A roaring lion.

411. Getting a camel through the eye of a needle.
412. Voice.
413. A bear.
414. A lion.
415. A lamb.

TIME

416. Two.
417. The days are shortened.
418. The third hour.
419. One thousand years.
420. About three hours.
421. Three-years.
422. Thirty-eight years.
423. The world began.
424. Twelve years.
425. The evil thereof.
426. Three months.
427. The last day of the feast.
428. Forty-two months.
429. One day.
430. His hour had not yet come.
431. The seventh hour.
432. The first, or Sunday.
433. Three days.
434. The Sabbath.
435. Rise again.
436. The restitution of all things.

BODY PARTS

437. The tongue.
438. Judas Iscariot.
439. The right hand.
440. The Father's.
441. Michael and the devil.
442. James 3.
443. The hem of Christ's garment.
444. The eye.
445. Touched them.
446. They gnashed on him with their teeth.
447. Pluck it out.
448. The god of this world, or the devil.
449. Ointment of spikenard.

450. "I have no need of thee."

EASY TRIVIA

451. Sitting at receipt of custom.
452. One.
453. Matthew 6.
454. Luke 3.
455. A Christian.
456. The judgment seat.
457. Our heart.
458. An holy kiss.
459. Heal him, cure him, or cast the evil spirit out.
460. Paul.
461. Righteous.
462. Joseph of Arimathaea.
463. Evil.
464. He hid it
465. The Lord.
466. A prisoner.

DOCTRINE

467. Baptism.
468. Faith.
469. Experience.
470. The Lord.
471. Jesus Christ.
472. The feebleminded.
473. Death.
474. Faith.
475. Jesus Christ.
476. Faith.
477. The righteous.
478. A "stumbling block."
479. Jesus Christ.
480. Promise.
481. God and mammon.
482. Galatians 4.
483. Sound doctrine.

FORGIVENESS

484. Seven.
485. He wrote on the ground.
486. Blasphemy.

487. He who has been trespassed against.
488. Stone.
489. Till seven times seventy.

PRAYER

490. A trance.
491. Wisdom.
492. Ceasing.
493. The friend at midnight.
494. Upbraid them.
495. Wavering.
496. A Publican.
497. All things.
498. The Pharisee.

FAITH

499. Galatians 3.
500. Hebrews 11.
501. All things.
502. A mountain.
503. The Centurion.
504. Works.
505. The "stumbling stone."
506. The Holy Spirit of Promise.
507. A mustard seed.
508. The shield.
509. The Law of Moses.

COMMANDMENTS

510. Melchizedek.
511. Tradition.
512. Love.
513. Be not angry with your brother.
514. Baptize.
515. Two.
516. "Corban."
517. To love thy neighbor as thyself.
518. Honor thy father and mother.
519. To love God.
520. Come forth.

ARMOR OF GOD

521. The wiles of the devil.
522. Truth.

523. Righteousness.
524. Gospel.
525. Faith.
526. Salvation.
527. The word of God.
528. Perseverance, Supplication.

SABBATH

529. A sinner.
530. Blameless.
531. Lord.
532. Spices and ointments.
533. Circumcision.
534. They wanted to destroy Him.
535. Because they were plucking and eating corn, or rubbing it between their hands.

SACRAMENT

536. During the Last Supper.
537. Ourselves.
538. Weak, sick, sleep (or die).
539. Blood.
540. The Lord's body.
541. The body and blood of the Lord.
542. Despise, shame.

BAPTISM

543. Three thousand.
544. John the Baptist.
545. To be tempted of the devil.
546. The Ethiopian eunuch.
547. The Holy Ghost.
548. John forbade Him.
549. The dead.
550. "This is my beloved Son."
551. The Holy Ghost, or Spirit of God.
552. It was to fulfill all righteousness.

SALVATION

553. Fear and trembling.
554. The Jews.
555. Boast.
556. Election.
557. Gift.

558. Silver and gold.
559. Strait and narrow.
560. Incorruption.
561. Faith.
562. The righteous.
563. Eternal Salvation.
564. Lose it.
565. Grace.

DEFINITIONS

566. Talithacumi.
567. Sexual lust.
568. "Be opened."
569. Temptations.
570. An escape.
571. The poison of asps.
572. Good manners.
573. Sin.
574. The hireling.
575. He pays for them.
576. Faith, hope, and charity.
577. Life.
578. The Holy Ghost.
579. Little children.
580. "My God, my God, why has thou forsaken me?"

PUNISHMENT

581. Darkness.
582. They beat them.
583. Five.
584. The marks of the Lord Jesus.
585. Shake the dust from their feet.
586. Stripes.
587. Tree.
588. Paul.
589. Outer darkness.
590. Eternal life.
591. The Jews.
592. A fig tree.
593. Blindness.
594. The Holy Ghost.
595. Unbelief.
596. Death.
597. The Bridegroom.

598. Our temple, or body.

SIN

599. Bulls and goats, or animal sacrifices.
600. Ignorantly, in unbelief.
601. Condemn her.
602. The law.
603. Death.
604. Death.
605. The one sick with palsy.
606. Righteousness.
607. The parents, or the man.
608. Law.

LIES

609. The Holy Ghost.
610. Satan's.
611. The price of property, or money.
612. Hypocrisy.
613. Money.

DISCOURSES

614. The Sermon on the Mount.
615. Many disciples left Jesus.
616. John 8.
617. A devil.
618. The good shepherd.
619. Judas (not Iscariot).
620. Capernaum.
621. They were pricked in their heart.
622. John 6.

GOSPEL

623. By revelation.
624. The Gentiles.
625. The fatherless.
626. The Gentiles.
627. Judged.
628. Peter and John.
629. An angel.
630. Paul.
631. Faith.
632. Crucify Him anew.
633. Shame.

BEATITUDES

634. The kingdom of heaven.
635. Comfort.
636. Earth.
637. Filled.
638. Mercy.
639. They shall see God.
640. The children of God.
641. The kingdom of heaven.
642. The prophets.
643. The pure in heart.

SERMON ON THE MOUNT

644. Do good to them.
645. Lord, Lord.
646. Our Father in heaven.
647. Those who mourn.
648. The lilies of the field.
649. Those that hunger and thirst after righteousness.
650. The golden rule.
651. They were astonished.
652. The just and the unjust, or good and evil.

GIFTS

653. 1 Corinthians 14.
654. Five.
655. The laying on of hands.
656. A widow.
657. One's self, or the speaker.
658. The interpretation of tongues.
659. Prophesies.
660. Tongues.
661. The gifts of the Spirit.
662. Gold, frankincense, and myrrh.
663. Judas Iscariot.
664. Eternal life.

TEMPLE

665. Sign.
666. A Greek.
667. Cast out the money changers.
668. The veil of the temple.

669. The Holy Ghost.
670. A scourge of cords, or a whip.
671. Simeon.
672. His body.
673. A den of thieves.
674. The tables of the money changers.
675. Twelve.
676. A beating.
677. It would be destroyed.

MIRACLES

678. By word only, or from a distance.
679. Silver and gold.
680. The coin in the mouth of the fish.
681. They could not cast a devil out of a child.
682. The second "drought" of fish.
683. Go with him.
684. The Sabbath.
685. They were healed.
686. The Son of God.
687. Peter.
688. "Wilt thou be made whole?"
689. The first "drought" of fish.

FOOD AND DRINK

690. Broiled fish and honeycomb.
691. Eating without washing.
692. Withered away, or died.
693. Two hundred pennyworth.
694. The Passover.
695. The word of righteousness.
696. The Passover.
697. His blood.
698. Why Jesus' disciples did not fast.

MONEY AND RICHES

699. The Kingdom of God.
700. Evil.
701. Sorrows.
702. Peter.
703. Lusts.
704. In the mouth of the fish.
705. Riches.
706. Nothing.

707. Sell all that he had.
708. "Who then can be saved?"
709. One.
710. Two mites, or a farthing.
711. James 5.
712. Philip.
713. The tormentors.
714. A Potters field.
715. A penny.

TRUST AND BELIEF

716. Devils.
717. Divisions, offenses.
718. Fables.
719. God.
720. Not.
721. Spirits.
722. King Herod.
723. Born again.
724. Teachers.
725. Science.
726. Priest.
727. Disorderly.

LOVE

728. Saints.
729. Nothing.
730. Giver.
731. The world.
732. Money.
733. Esau.
734. He "chasteneth," or chastens.
735. Brother.
736. Mother and father, son and daughter.
737. His commandments.

DEATH

738. Eutychus.
739. To the spirit prison.
740. The twinkling of an eye.
741. Sin.
742. Bread, Cup.
743. Lazarus.
744. Crucifixion.

745. Eutychus.
746. With a sword.
747. Christ.
748. The devil.
749. The voice of Jesus.
750. Gain.
751. A Roman centurion.
752. Stones.
753. Herod.

JUDGMENT AND REWARD

754. My Father.
755. Righteous judgment.
756. The Son, or Jesus Christ.
757. The east and west.
758. They shook the dust from their feet.
759. So that we will not be judged.
760. "What shall we have therefore?"
761. Two or three.
762. Five thousand.
763. Jesus Christ.
764. The Father, or God.
765. He was made a ruler over many things.
766. Our righteousness.
767. Both God and Christ.
768. Celestial and terrestrial.
769. Earth.

PARABLES

770. The Son of Man.
771. He fared sumptuously every day.
772. All.
773. One hundred pence.
774. Whatever was right.
775. I will go, but went not.
776. They beat, stoned, and killed them.
777. The Unmerciful Servant.
778. "Lest . . . she weary me."
779. The first person, or the one with ten talents.
780. "The children of the wicked one."
781. For some of their oil.
782. The wicked one.

783. I will not, but afterward he repented, and went.
784. Outer darkness.
785. The Laborers in the Vineyard.
786. The unjust steward.
787. "Who is my neighbor?"
788. Wedding garments.
789. The great supper, or marriage supper.

AND PARABLES AGAIN

790. Five.
791. All refused to come.
792. On good ground.
793. The parable of the Pounds.
794. The fowls.
795. Tribulation and persecution.
796. It fell in the thorns.
797. Cares of the world and the deceitfulness of riches.
798. The son.
799. The field.

ORGANIZATION

800. Good men, hospitality.
801. Saints.
802. The synagogue.
803. Seven.
804. Stephen.
805. Last.
806. Timothy.
807. Anoint with oil.
808. Edify it.
809. Philip.
810. Doubletongued.
811. Teach.
812. A double honor.
813. A novice.

KNOW THE APOSTLES

814. Thaddaeus, Lebbaeus, Judas.
815. Thomas.
816. James and John.
817. Judas Iscariot.
818. Philip.

819. Peter and Andrew.
820. Matthias.
821. Simon Zelotes.
822. James.
823. Matthew Levi.
824. Nathanael.
825. Paul

MORE ABOUT APOSTLES

826. John, or the disciple Jesus loved.
827. The keys of the kingdom.
828. Jesus Christ.
829. He put them in prison.
830. Peter.
831. About one hundred and twenty.
832. Peter.
833. Peter.
834. Peter.
835. Jesus Christ.
836. Worshiped Jesus.
837. John, or the disciple Jesus loved.
838. Killing them.
839. The second Simon.
840. They "marvelled."
841. The House of Israel.
842. Paul.

OCCUPATIONS

843. A publican.
844. He was a sorcerer.
845. A physician.
846. That of a carpenter.
847. Paul.
848. They were fishers, or fisherman.
849. Fishers of men.

PENTECOST

850. They heard in their own tongue, or "interpretation of tongues."
851. Christ's resurrection.
852. David.
853. A rushing wind.
854. Peter.
855. Drunk or full of wine.
856. The gift of tongues.

857. The healing of the lame man.
858. Joel.
859. Cloven tongues of fire.
860. All things.

PROCEDURE

861. Witnesses.
862. Planted.
863. James.
864. The elders.
865. Before the world began.
866. The water and the Spirit.
867. Oil.
868. Envying and/or strife.
869. Exalted.
870. Filthy lucre, or money.
871. Doers.

PRIESTHOOD

872. The Law.
873. Juda or Judah.
874. Aaron.
875. The Levitical Priesthood.
876. Melchizedek.
877. Peculiar.

ANGELS

878. Gabriel.
879. "A trumpet."
880. In a dream.
881. Michael.
882. Dead men.
883. Strangers.
884. One-third.
885. Sins.
886. Lightning.
887. Satan, or the devil.
888. "He is risen."
889. Gospel.
890. Hell.
891. One hundred and forty-four thousand.
892. Their first estate.

PRISON

893. Two years.
894. Felix.
895. An earthquake.
896. The house of Mary, the mother of John Mark.
897. Two years.
898. An angel.
899. An angel.
900. Your adversary.
901. His own hired house.
902. The jailer.
903. The Lord.
904. The Gentiles.

MULTIPLE CHOICE

905. Remembrance.
906. Fourth.
907. Six.
908. An angel.
909. Ten thousand talents.
910. Five.
911. A trumpet.
912. Extra oil.
913. Fear.
914. Forty-two.
915. "Lambs."
916. Reward.
917. At Antioch.
918. Two.
919. Advocate.
920. Debts.
921. Seven.
922. Spiritually.
923. Understand.
924. Three.
925. John Mark.
926. Once.
927. Twelve hundred and sixty days.

NEW TESTAMENT TRIVIA

928. "The Acts of the Apostles."
929. Matthew, Mark, and Luke.

930. "The Epistle of Paul the Apostle to the Colossians."
931. "The Second Epistle of Paul the Apostle to the Corinthians."
932. "The Epistle of Paul the Apostle to the Ephesians."
933. Amen.
934. One.
935. "The First Epistle of Paul the Apostle to the Thessalonians."
936. One.
937. "The Second Epistle of John."
938. One.
939. It is the Bible's shortest verse.
940. One.
941. "The Revelation of St. John the Divine."
942. Chapter 4, verse 8.
943. "Jesus wept."
944. "The General Epistle of James."
945. "The Epistle of Paul the Apostle to the Romans."
946. "The New Testament of our Lord and Saviour Jesus Christ."
947. Twenty-eight.

Numbers Games

948. Five.
949. Five.
950. Five.
951. Five.
952. Seventy.
953. Twenty-four.
954. Five.
955. Ninety-nine.
956. Four.
957. Four.
958. Four days.
959. Four.
960. Sixteen.
961. Three.
962. Fourteen.
963. Over forty.
964. Four.
965. Six.

966. Twenty-one.
967. The eleventh hour.
968. Three.
969. Above five hundred.

Numbers Square

970. Sixteen.
971. Five.
972. Three.
973. Seven.
974. Thirteen.
975. Three.
976. Sixteen.
977. One.
978. Thirteen.
979. Two.
980. Ten.
981. Four.
982. Twelve.
983. Eight.
984. Three.
985. One.
986. Twelve.
987. Twenty-eight.
988. Ten.
989. One.
990. Eighteen.

Gospels Trivia

991. Philip.
992. Nazareth.
993. Lazarus.
994. The Lord's prayer.
995. Capernaum.
996. Fourteen.
997. The pool at Bethesda.
998. A master.
999. A pound.
1000. A cave.
1001. A great gulf.
1002. "The Gospel According to St. Matthew."
1003. His nets.
1004. The sinners.
1005. The generation.

1006. Mark.

EPISTLES TRIVIA

1007. "The Second Epistle of Paul the Apostle to Timothy."
1008. "The First Epistle of Paul the Apostle to the Corinthians."
1009. Two.
1010. One.
1011. Rome.
1012. Rome.
1013. In Rome.
1014. Silvanus and Thimotheus (Timothy).
1015. Timotheus (Timothy).
1016. Two.
1017. "The General Epistle of Jude."
1018. "The Epistle of Paul the Apostle to the Philippians."
1019. One.
1020. Rome.
1021. To "The Elect lady and her children."
1022. "The Third Epistle of John."
1023. Rome.
1024. "The Second Epistle of Paul the Apostle to the Thessalonians."
1025. "The Epistle of Paul to Philemon."
1026. "The Epistle of Paul to Titus."
1027. "The First Epistle of Paul the Apostle to Timothy."
1028. "The Epistle of Paul the Apostle to the Hebrews."
1029. One.
1030. "The Second Epistle General of Peter."
1031. All in Galatia.
1032. "The First Epistle General of Peter."
1033. "The First Epistle General of John."
1034. One.
1035. Athens.

FILL IN THE BLANK

1036. Perfect, perfect.
1037. Worse.
1038. Water, wine.
1039. Firstborn.
1040. Respect.
1041. Light.
1042. "Asunder."
1043. Worship.
1044. Vengeance, repay.
1045. Gods, lords.
1046. Gall, iniquity.
1047. Letter, spirit.
1048. Hunger, thirst.
1049. Loose.
1050. Crown.
1051. Thorns, thistles.
1052. Gnat, camel.
1053. Trample.
1054. Circumcision nor uncircumcision.
1055. "Denying."
1056. Rejoice.
1057. Strengthened.
1058. Spirit, flesh.
1059. Commandments.
1060. Man, man.
1061. Romans.
1062. "Fire."
1063. Son.
1064. Word.
1065. "Good fight."
1066. Faith, love, hope.
1067. Seen.
1068. New.
1069. "Finished my course."
1070. "Good."
1071. Wars, wars.
1072. "Kindleth."
1073. Signs, wonders.
1074. Few.
1075. Substance, evidence.
1076. Easy, light.
1077. Ears, tongue.
1078. Victory.

1079. Things, things.
1080. Heaven, men.
1081. Philosophy, deceit.
1082. Sabbath, Sabbath.
1083. Weeping.

SCRIPTURE

1084. Doctrine, reproof, correction, instruction.
1085. John 4:2.
1086. Perfect.
1087. Wrest them.
1088. Esaias, (Isaiah).
1089. Esaias, or Isaiah.
1090. Eternal life.
1091. Jesus.
1092. The angels.
1093. Book.
1094. The raising of Lazarus.
1095. Inspiration.
1096. Interpretation.

GEOGRAPHY

1097. World.
1098. Jacob's well.
1099. Mars Hill.
1100. Prophet.
1101. John the Baptist.
1102. The sheep market.
1103. The world.
1104. Galilee.
1105. Bethesda.
1106. A Nobleman.
1107. Galilee.
1108. In Galilee.
1109. Galilee.
1110. The field of blood.
1111. Fulness.
1112. Aenon.

WORLD

1113. Rejoice.
1114. Evil.
1115. The Saints.
1116. Sin.

1117. The Father's.
1118. Soul.
1119. Death.
1120. Nothing.
1121. The light.
1122. Foolishness.
1123. Wax cold.
1124. Foreordained.
1125. Tribulation.
1126. Chosen.
1127. Peace.

ROCKS

1128. Offence.
1129. Paul.
1130. Jesus Christ.
1131. Cut himself.
1132. Stephen.
1133. Christ.
1134. Children of Abraham.
1135. "Lord, by this time he stinketh," or "He stinketh."
1136. The head of the corner.
1137. Sinless.
1138. An angel.

WEATHER

1139. Fair.
1140. The whole house.
1141. Lowering.
1142. An angel.
1143. Sleeping.
1144. The wind.
1145. They marveled.
1146. The wind.
1147. A talent.
1148. A great calm.
1149. Three years, six months.
1150. Rain, floods, and wind.
1151. "Euroclydon."
1152. Rain, floods, and wind.
1153. Signs.
1154. Red.

GEOGRAPHY MAP

1155. Galiloo.
1156. Egypt.
1157. Cilicia.
1158. Crete.
1159. Asia.
1160. Athens.
1161. The Sea of Tiberias.
1162. Syria.
1163. Jericho.
1164. Melita (modern name: Malta)
1165. Iconium.

JERUSALEM

1166. About fifteen furlongs.
1167. Troubled.
1168. Tree branches.
1169. The sun and moon.
1170. Bethphage.
1171. Two hundred thousand thousand or two hundred million.
1172. A prophet.
1173. Fourteen.
1174. Dust.
1175. King.
1176. Garments and branches.
1177. The glory of God and the Lamb.
1178. Rome.
1179. Caesar.
1180. Hosanna.

UNIVERSE

1181. Angels.
1182. Stars.
1183. Evil.
1184. Barnabas.
1185. The heavens.
1186. The sun, moon, and stars.
1187. The sun and moon.

HARD TRIVIA

1188. The Twelve tribes.
1189. Luke 2:52.
1190. Treasures.

1191. "Damsel, I say unto thee, arise.".
1192. Unknown, unrecorded.
1193. The Feast of Tabernacles.
1194. "Sir, I perceive that thou art a prophet."
1195. Spirit.
1196. Dionysius the Areopagite.
1197. 1 Corinthians 12.
1198. Babes.
1199. Chapter 5 (Gal. 5:19–21).
1200. Matthew 7:12.
1201. Chapter 3 (Col. 3:8–19).
1202. Romans 13.

JEWS

1203. The Passover.
1204. Widow's houses.
1205. Their traditions.
1206. Because the Jews sought to kill Him.
1207. Their phylacteries.
1208. The Sadducees.
1209. A sign.
1210. Our place and nation.
1211. Kill himself.
1212. Jesus.
1213. Their sins.
1214. A stumbling block.
1215. The Herodians.
1216. God.
1217. The first one in the water.

GENTILES

1218. Jesus Christ.
1219. Cornelius.
1220. He was a Centurion.
1221. Palsy.
1222. The Holy Ghost.
1223. Two hours.
1224. The Pharisees.
1225. The elders of the Jews.
1226. The Jews.
1227. He worshiped him.
1228. The centurion.
1229. Paul.

1230. A word.

NAMES TRIVIA

1231. Judas and Silas.
1232. Hymenaeus and Philetus.
1233. Alphaeus.
1234. Timotheus (Timothy) and Silvanus.
1235. Barjesus.
1236. Alphaeus.
1237. Rhoda.
1238. Trophimus.
1239. Annas.
1240. Apollos.
1241. Damaris.
1242. Julius.
1243. Peter.
1244. Publius.
1245. Simon.
1246. Thimotheus, (Timothy).
1247. Pontius.
1248. Justus.
1249. Dorcas.
1250. "The field of blood."
1251. Barsabas.
1252. Boanerges.
1253. Silas.
1254. In the opinion of most scholars: Lebbaeus and Thaddaeus.

TRUE/FALSE

1255. False (Good).
1256. True.
1257. True.
1258. False, (Capernaum).
1259. True.
1260. False (of the Pharisees and Sadducees).
1261. False, (over the body of Moses).
1262. False (one flesh).
1263. False (loveth himself).
1264. True.
1265. True.
1266. False, (at home).
1267. True.

1268. False (for bringing little children).
1269. True.
1270. True.
1271. False (Lusts).
1272. True.
1273. True.
1274. True.
1275. False, (the truth).
1276. True.
1277. False, (charity).
1278. True.
1279. False (the whole have no need of a physician).
1280. False (should assist one overtaken in a fault).
1281. True.
1282. False, (the shedding of blood).
1283. True.
1284. False (foolish and unlearned questions gender strife).

FINALE

1285. The daughter of Herodias is not identified by name in the New Testament. There has been speculation that her name is Salome, and that has even been provided by a genealogical family tree by some researchers identifying her as the daughter of Herodias and Philip (Herod Antipas' brother); but her name (considered Christian mythology by some) is not revealed in the New Testament records. Some in history have given Oscar Wilde credit for first naming her. He used the name in his 19th century play, first published in 1893. Multiple works have been done since that time, all using the name Salome.

TRICK QUESTIONS

1286. He was Transfigured.
1287. Steal.

Challenged by the New Testament

1288. One.
1289. His eyes.
1290. Christ.
1291. The Golden Rule.
1292. Timothy.
1293. That they have no wine, or had run out of wine.
1294. Abraham.
1295. Law.
1296. Baptism.
1297. The Epistle of Paul from Laodicea.
1298. Colosse.
1299. "The Epistle of Paul the Apostle to the Galatians."
1300. Mercy.
1301. Two.

1302. Four.
1303. Against Him.
1304. The last.
1305. Sleep.
1306. Prisoner.
1307. The name of Jesus Christ.
1308. Hope.
1309. None.
1310. World, world.
1311. Five thousand.
1312. Corinth.
1313. The wicked husbandmen.
1314. Truth.
1315. Many.
1316. Thessalonians.
1317. None.